THE LEGAL PR
1992

THE IVANHOE/BLACKSTONE GUIDE TO

THE LEGAL PROFESSION
1992

Edited by

Sarah Jackson
Gill Zacharous

Published in association with
BLACKSTONE PRESS

First published 1992
by Charles Letts & Co Ltd
Letts of London House
Parkgate Road
London SW11 4NQ
Tel: 071-407 8891
Fax: 071-407 5357
© 1992 Charles Letts & Co Ltd

Associate publisher
   Blackstone Press Limited
   9–15 Aldine Street
   London W12 8AW
   Tel: 081-740 1173
   Fax: 081-743 2292

All rights reserved. No part of this publication may be reproduced, stored in a retrieval system or transmitted, in any form or by any means, electronic, mechanical, photocopying, recording or otherwise without the prior permission of the copyright owner.

ISBN 1 85238 4603
ISSN 0955-7172

While every effort has been made to ensure its accuracy, no responsibility for loss occasioned to any person acting or refraining from action as a result of any material in this publication can be accepted by the publisher or authors.

Illustrated by Danny Byrne, Tony Holland and Nick Newman.
Typeset by Anneset, Weston-super-Mare, Avon.
Printed and bound in Great Britain.

British Library Cataloguing in Publication Data
A catalogue record for this book is available from the British Library

Contents

Foreword – *The Lord Chancellor*..*ix*

Part I: An overview of the legal profession

A brief history of the legal profession – *Gary Scanlan*......................3
Solicitors – *Jenny Goddard*..7
The modern Bar – *David Latham QC*..13
Legal executives – *Ian Watson*..17

Part II: The law degree

Why read law? – *Gary Scanlan*..23
Where to study law – *Bob Lee*..27
Preparation for the course – *Christopher Ryan*..................................31

Part III: Becoming a solicitor

Routes into the profession – *Richard Ramsay*....................................37
The formal training and examinations – *Colin Beatty*......................43
Training within a large firm – *Tom Purton*..47
Articles within the smaller firm – *Paul Trim*......................................51
Notes on qualifying as a solicitor...54
Information and statistics...59

Part IV: The qualified career

Legal careers – a general overview – *Katrina Smith*..........................69
Company and commercial law – *Jonathan Elstein*............................73
Practising in planning law – *Elaine A Driver*....................................75
Criminal law – *David Savage*..79
Working overseas – *Simon Martin*..81
A career in taxation – *John Avery Jones*..85
The work of an intellectual property solicitor – *Mark Lubbock*......87

v

Private client work in a large firm – *Justin Appleyard* 90
A legal career in commerce, finance and industry – *Kamlesh Bahl* 93
Working in a legal aid practice – *Roberta Tish* 97
The Government Legal Service 101
The Crown Prosecution Service – *Graeme McKerrell* 103
The lawyer in local government – *Helmut Cartwright* 107
The Magistrates' Courts Service – *Stephen Caven* 113
Working at a law centre – *Melody Pavey* 117
Transferring from the Law Society to the Bar 119
Information and statistics 120

Part V: Becoming a barrister

What does a barrister do? 129
Routes into the profession – *Susan Blake* 131
The formal training – the Vocational Course and the Bar Examination – *Susan Blake* 137
Pupillage and the practical training – *David Latham QC* 143

Part VI: The qualified career

The Criminal Bar 149
The Family Law Bar 150
The Chancery Bar 151
The Revenue Bar 152
The London Common Law and Commercial Bar Association 153
The Commercial Bar Association (COMBAR) 154
The Patent Bar 155
The Administrative Law Bar 156
The Local Government and Planning Bar 157
Official referees and the Bar 158
Barristers in commerce, finance and industry – *David Fletcher Rogers* 159
Transferring from the Bar to the Law Society 165

Part VII: The directory

How to select a firm of solicitors 169
Using the directory 173

The Law Society Careers & Recruitment Service 174
Allen & Overy 176
Ashurst Morris Crisp 178
Beachcroft Stanleys 181
Berwin Leighton 182
S J Berwin & Co 184
Cameron Markby Hewitt 185
Eversheds 186
Frere Cholmeley 189
Herbert Smith 190
Lovell White Durrant 192
Nabarro Nathanson 194
Slaughter and May 196
Taylor Willcocks 198
Titmuss Sainer & Webb 199
Turner Kenneth Brown 200
Watson, Farley & Williams 201
Wilde Sapte 202

Foreword

When a book is published in 1992, it is only right that some reference be made to the significance of this year as we move towards closer integration with our European partners. While there is still a healthy level of debate as to the form of this closer cooperation, what is now widely accepted is that progress will be made and that the legal profession will play a leading role in the complex negotiations ahead.

Yet this is just one example of an area in which Great Britain relies on its legal profession. Many others exist – such as the drafting of legislation that may affect all our lives for many years, the provision of legal advice to the less well-off, the staffing of many senior posts in industry and commerce and the practical advice that ensures our economy and society develop in an orderly fashion, in accordance with a body of law that evolves and adjusts to changing needs.

Much of this we take for granted, but in fact it relies almost entirely on the high calibre of the individuals who make up both branches of the legal profession. If a career full of challenge, hard work and responsibility does not appeal to you then you should not attempt to become a lawyer. If, however, such a career does appeal to you and you wish to promote justice in its many facets, then I recommend it to you as an opportunity few young people today are offered in other fields.

Mackay of Clashfern

The Right Honourable Lord Mackay of Clashfern
The Lord Chancellor

Part I
An overview of the legal profession

A brief history of the legal profession
GARY SCANLAN

Gary Scanlan qualified as a Solicitor and is currently a Lecturer in Law at an English university. He has published numerous articles and reviews in professional legal journals and is the Consultant Editor of *The Legal Executive.* **He is the coauthor of** *An Introduction to Criminal Law, SWOT Criminal Law* **and** *A Guide to the Criminal Justice Act 1988,* **all published by Blackstone Press.**

Whenever society creates a need, the expert who can satisfy that need follows. The law is no exception. With the coming of the Norman conquest a ruthless plundering of the riches of the nation began. The Norman kings were interested in strong central government, as this was a necessity if the wealth of the nation was to be effectively exploited. They came across a land where each county and even village ran its affairs based upon local custom and practice. In the early Middle Ages local courts using local custom settled disputes between neighbours without recourse to recognized principles of law. It became a practice for the Angevin kings to send representatives (frequently clerics) to these courts and gradually they began to adopt and impose the customs of particular courts they had visited, and of which they approved, to all such courts. These officials from the King's Court began to develop these nationally applied rules into a systematic set of legal principles that would become the common law, and in doing so created both the King's Court (the Common Law Courts) and constituted themselves a professional judiciary. All this was completed by the middle of the thirteenth century. These national courts began to dispense a system of justice that was superior to the local courts. They provided both a means of aiding the centralization of government and a source of profit to the Crown. The judges received fees from litigants and in criminal cases, persons convicted by the King's judges of serious offences, known as felonies, forfeited both their lives and their property to the King. The King's Courts also enforced the King's rights as the ultimate feudal landlord.

These first judges were recruited from among the clerks in the Royal

Household and the Chancery (the department of the Royal Household responsible for the preparing and issuing of the King's Writs). These King's judges are the ancestors of the modern High Court judges. Eventually, the medieval judges would be recruited from the successful advocates who practised in the King's Courts.

There were in the Middle Ages three common law courts, each staffed by its own judges and court officials, the courts of King's Bench, Common Pleas, and the Court of Exchequer. Each of these courts had originally an exclusive jurisdiction, but in seeking to extend their 'business' and their fees the judiciary of each of these courts so extended their original jurisdictions that they became indistinguishable from one another, at least as regards the types of cases they would hear.

In each of the courts there were two distinct sets of legal practitioners. There were those who told or narrated the litigant's story in court and those who in the absence of the litigant represented and advised him. At that time all steps in an action had to take place in one of the King's Courts and in the presence of the litigant or his representative.

The 'narrators' would become the modern barristers. In the course of time the narrators formed themselves into two distinct grades. The ablest and foremost of them constituting themselves the order of 'Serjeants at Law', the others formed the societies that we now know as the Inns of Court. These 'Serjeants at Law', the most eminent of advocates appointed by patents from the King, were the body of men from whom the judges of the King's Courts were appointed. They had an exclusive right of audience in the most prominent and prestigious of the King's Courts, the Court of Common Pleas. As the other common law courts fought for their share of litigants' fees, the Court of Common Pleas and the 'Serjeant at Law' diminished in importance until the passing of the Judicature Acts 1873–1875 reorganized the common law courts on the modern footing. From this date, it was no longer necessary for a barrister to be a 'Serjeant at Law' to be appointed a High Court judge (the latter term coming into use from that time). The 'Serjeant at Law' ceased to be.

The junior branch of the barristers' profession regulated themselves and though originally known as 'apprentices' grew in prestige and importance. It was found from the end of the sixteenth century that the law offices of the Attorney and Solicitor General (originally the King's Lawyers) required assistance in conducting legal affairs on behalf of the Crown and the State. Barristers of suitable political sympathies were appointed 'King's Council' and were obliged to place their services at the disposal of the King and the Government. This is the origin of the modern QC.

The practitioners who represented the litigant and who advised him generally were attached to each of the common law courts; they were constituted officers of the court to which they were attached and their profession of attorney at law was regulated by the judges of that court. One rival court system to the common law courts which grew up was the Court of Chancery. This court dealt with cases involving property, wills and probate and the application of the body of legal rules that would become known as the rules of equity. Though this court was staffed by legal clerks who were supposed to advise litigants they were held in disrepute. A class of men came into being who acted on behalf of litigants in the Court of Chancery, and who tried to ensure that their clients' interests were promoted, and since they solicited the interests of their clients they became known as 'solicitors'. Eventually this profession was recognized as being the equal of the profession of attorney in any of the common law courts.

In the eighteenth century the branches of these professions of attorney and solicitor formed an association called the Society of Gentleman Practisers in the Courts of Law and Equity, a voluntary association which attorneys, solicitors and a profession known as proctors (individuals who practised amongst other things in the Ecclesiastical Courts) could join. Attorneys frequently became attorneys in each of the three common law courts and on occasion were also admitted as solicitors and vice versa. In 1831, the Society of Gentleman Practisers and other smaller and similar associations formed themselves into the Law Society. This body, though a voluntary association, now regulates the training and conduct of the professional lawyer who is now known as a solicitor. In 1875, with the passing of the Judicature Acts, the common law courts and the Courts of Chancery were amalgamated into the modern High Court. Though at the time the High Court consisted of five divisions, today there are only three divisions of the High Court: the Queen's Bench, the Family and the Chancery division. The professions of attorney and solicitor were, from 1875, practically assimilated. The Law Society had to choose a name for the profession and the practitioners, who could now practise law and give general legal advice and represent the interests of litigants in all the divisions of the High Court. Inexplicably ignoring the more noble and distinguished name of the practitioners of the old common law courts, the Law Society selected the less flattering name of solicitor to describe and name the profession. The modern professions of both barristers and solicitors, the nature of the work they now undertake, their likely futures and a discussion of the differences between these two branches of the legal profession are discussed in the articles that follow.

Solicitors
JENNY GODDARD

Jenny Goddard has been a careers adviser in higher education for several years and is currently Careers Promotion Officer for the Law Society.

The solicitors' profession offers variety and challenge to all who enter it. There are over 55,000 solicitors in England and Wales, and the work that they do varies almost as much as the individuals within it. Whatever your skills, abilities, interests or personality type, there is something to suit you in the solicitors' profession.

What is the role of a solicitor?

The specific duty of a solicitor is to serve his or her client with skilled legal advice and representation. Clients can range from the individual making his or her will or buying a house, to the large corporation negotiating a multimillion pound deal, and the role of the solicitor varies accordingly. For instance, if you choose a career as a solicitor, you could well find yourself using your knowledge of the law to negotiate a complex deal between two overseas companies, or putting together a defence in a major crime trial.

The solicitors' profession is expanding in accordance with the demands on it. More and more people are using the services of solicitors and the advice of the profession is increasingly in demand. The advice can be about buying houses, selling companies, defending crimes or acquiring a divorce. It is a career choice which combines an interest in the law with the ability to work with and for people, intellectual stimulus and a huge amount of variety.

Where do solicitors work?

There are three main areas of work for solicitors; private practice, local and central government, and commerce and industry.

Private practice

By far the majority of solicitors (over eighty per cent) work in private practice and approximately ninety per cent of trainee solicitors enter private practice. This is a business partnership of solicitors who come together to offer a service to their clients. If you were to join such a firm you would start as a trainee solicitor, become an assistant solicitor when qualified, and eventually work towards becoming a partner, thus sharing in the management and profits of the business. The type of work done by such firms varies enormously.

Firms range in size from vast partnerships (usually in the City of London and similar areas) right down to the sole practitioner in high street practices all over the country. They also vary in terms of the services they provide and the clients they serve. In a general practice, you would find between, say, six to a dozen partners who offer a range of services. The small, sole practitioner may concentrate on offering a service in conveyancing and probate. Many firms of solicitors concentrate on legal aid work, offering a service to those whose income does not allow them to pay for the services of a solicitor. The work here can concentrate on areas such as matrimonial, housing, social security, welfare and other related matters. At the other end of the spectrum, there are firms in the City of London and in the business areas of other large towns such as Birmingham, Bristol, Manchester, Norwich and elsewhere who offer a service predominantly to business or corporate clients. These tend to be very large organizations and often have branch offices throughout the world. They would concentrate on the services available to the larger business and often have very specialist areas of work.

In general practice, you could be providing a broad range of services to local people, dealing with such matters as divorce and child care, conveyancing and property work, consumer and business law and also with housing or social security problems. Many general practices also have a crime department. The work is as much constructive as problem solving, such as helping a new business set up, drafting a complicated will or trust or drawing up forms of contract. This type of work can be very satisfying as it enables you to build up contacts with long-term clients and to serve the local small business community and private individuals.

Many firms and, indeed many solicitors, are tending to specialize increasingly. Obvious specialist areas are crime, shipping and insurance law, planning and construction work, financial services, social security law, etc. The choice here is what kind of client you see yourself dealing with and how you feel you can function best. Whatever appeals to you, whether it is a particular kind of expertise, or a particular type of firm, you will have the chance to develop your own skills within that area.

Local and central government
Several thousand solicitors are employed in local government, where their role is to provide advice on the important range of public services which a local authority offers; planning, transport, social services, leisure facilities, education and many others. There is an opportunity to specialize here and the chance to get involved with the local authority and to advise elected council members on policy matters. There is the opportunity for advocacy, such as appearing in court seeking an order for child care. A large number of solicitors who do not train in private practice train in local government.

All government departments employ solicitors as part of the civil service. Here, you could be involved in advising ministers on the implementation of government policy, drafting new legislation, or overseeing the implementation of existing legislation. This can be a fascinating career for someone who is interested in being involved in government as a whole.

The Crown Prosecution Service, which is the body responsible for prosecuting offenders on behalf of the police, is also a branch of the civil service which employs a huge number of solicitors. It is possible to train with the Crown Prosecution Service and for those who are interested in advocacy and crime this offers an interesting and varied career. If you join the Crown Prosecution Service, you would spend considerable time in court and in dealing with the policy connected with the prosecution of offenders, in itself a fascinating and complex area.

Commerce and industry
An increasing number of companies employ solicitors as 'in-house legal advisers'. Here the work is obviously commercially based; you would be using an acquired knowledge of company law and business structure, business and financial matters, and other related information for the successful running of the business of which you would be a part. Many legal departments in commerce and industry are small, enabling you to take a varied and wide ranging role within the business. There is a great deal of responsibility in such posts.

Other opportunities
Many solicitors work in law centres, which offer a less formal approach and service to the public, who are not charged for services. They are often open

at the weekends and in the evenings and offer opportunities for voluntary and part-time work by solicitors. It is also possible to work as a solicitor for a trade union, a charity or for other small organizations. Many work for the Magistrates' Courts Service and contribute to the running of our legal system.

Solicitors and international work

Many people are interested in knowing whether a career as a solicitor can involve them in international work or in Europe and the single market. Many solicitors' firms have traditionally had offices overseas, often in English speaking countries, such as the United States, Australia, the Far East and so on. With the approach of 1992, large numbers of firms opened offices in Western Europe; there are now many opportunities to work as a solicitor in the European financial centres and some firms have offices in Brussels, Paris, Dusseldorf, Frankfurt, Madrid and elsewhere. You will also find some firms opening offices in Eastern Europe and indeed in Japan. Others are forging different types of links, either by opening offices, or working in liaison with their European counterparts. If you are interested in working for such a firm, speak to your careers adviser or look into publications such as the Law Society's ROSET (Register of Solicitors Employing Trainees) for further information.

Under the 1991 EC Directive, solicitors may be able to qualify as lawyers within other European jurisdictions and this dual qualification will be extremely useful in the years to come.

How to qualify as a solicitor

The mechanics of qualification are discussed elsewhere in this book, but, apart from the question of passing the right examinations and getting through the training process, the people who are attracted to the profession are usually those with good communication skills, the ability to work under pressure and high academic ability. It should also be added that solicitors should have very high standards of integrity and a respect for the clients who come to them for help.

The future

The range of services solicitors supply is expanding all the time, as is the number of people using their services. Now, and in the next century, solicitors will be at the forefront of commercial, community and international life. In addition, the changes brought in by the Courts and Legal Services Act and other measures offer new opportunities to those who are about to qualify. If you would like to be a part of this exciting and dynamic profession, you will have an enormous range of choice and opportunity open to you.

Blackstone's
STATUTE BOOKS

Blackstone's Statute Books have been designed specifically with the law student in mind. Following extensive research, each book has been compiled to meet the needs of specific courses.

By selecting only essential material, we have been able to restrict both the size and the price of the books.

The books are ideal for use in examinations.

And the series covers most of the subjects studied on a law degree.

COMMERCIAL LAW STATUTES
F. Rose £11.95

CONTRACT AND TORT STATUTES
3rd Edn. F. Rose £9.95

CRIMINAL LAW STATUTES 2nd Edn.
P. Glazebrook £8.95

EEC LEGISLATION 2nd Edn.
N. Foster £11.95

EMPLOYMENT LAW STATUTES 2nd Edn.
R. Kidner £10.95

ENGLISH LEGAL SYSTEM STATUTES
D. Howarth and S. Wilson £11.95

EVIDENCE STATUTES
P. Huxley and M. O'Connell

FAMILY LAW STATUTES
M. Oldham £11.95

INTERNATIONAL LAW DOCUMENTS
M. Evans £12.95

LANDLORD AND TENANT STATUTES
S. Bridge £14.95

PROPERTY LAW STATUTES
M. Thomas £11.95

PUBLIC LAW STATUTES 2nd Edn.
P. Wallington and R. Lee £10.95

New titles to be published in 1992
INTELLECTUAL PROPERTY STATUTES
A. Christie

MEDICAL LAW STATUTES
M. Jones and A. Morris

PLANNING LAW STATUTES
V. Moore and D. Hughes

 BLACKSTONE PRESS LIMITED
9-15 ALDINE STREET, LONDON W12 8AW Tel: 081 740 1173 Fax: 081 743 2292

The modern Bar

DAVID LATHAM QC

David Latham is a QC practising in general common law in London. The former Chairman of the Bar's working party on pupillage which reported in 1988, he is currently the Chairman of the Professional Standards Committee of the Bar Council.

John Mortimer has much to answer for. Just when the Bar was trying to impress the world with its modern, forward thinking, computerized image, along comes Rumpole to spoil the picture. Crumpled, crusty, not at all contemporary, but thoroughly convivial, his image appears to cut across all the messages which the Bar's public relation advisers have been sending out to the public. The Bar which they seek to project is dedicated, professional, and properly equipped with all the modern technology which is necessary to provide a service to clients in the modern world.

Properly understood, Rumpole is the best argument for an independent Bar. He is in fact utterly professional; he is dedicated to achieving the best result for his client; he is wholly professional in his approach, particularly in court, where he ignores the judge, and concentrates entirely on the people who matter, the jury. Modern technology is of no interest to him, since it is of no relevance to the way he needs to do his work, for his clients. And his fierce independence would make it impossible for anyone to feel able to employ him, or join him in any comfortable partnership. There remains room at the Bar for people like him; the world would be a better place for more of them.

His importance is, however, for what he exemplifies, rather than for what he is. He is one example of the many facets of barrister which now make up the modern Bar. There are now over 7,000 barristers. They are all specialists in one form or another. A large proportion are specialists in advocacy pure and simple. But more and more, with the growing demands made by the sophistication of legislation, and the complexity of the business and financial world, the Bar provides what might be described as the double specialty, namely the advocate with specific expertise in a particular area of the law. The common factor is advocacy, and the common determination is

14 The modern Bar

to do the best for one's client. As a result, whilst Rumpole is able to provide the best for his client without modern technology by reason of the nature of his work, there are those who have to provide a service for government, the City, commerce and many other organizations, where the work requires the use of modern technology as an essential tool; and where it is essential, the Bar uses it.

The Bar is a consultancy profession. The barristers' clients are themselves professionals. As an independent practitioner you ultimately succeed or fail on your own merits, there will be no cushioning provided by others. It is therefore a very competitive profession, from the moment that the prospective barrister becomes a pupil, right through to the end of his career. For those who wish to succeed, it involves a lot of very hard work, often at antisocial hours. Above all, the raison d'être of the barrister, that is advocacy, whether at the highest levels, or indeed the lowest, requires an ability to thrive on adrenalin. Almost every appearance in court has similarities to an examination. And experienced barristers will tell you that the nerves before you go into court get no easier to bear however senior you become.

It is important to underline these fundamental features of a barrister's life before considering the way in which the modern Bar operates. There are specialist areas at the Bar in which court advocacy plays only a small part in the overall work of the barrister. But for the vast majority of the Bar, even the paperwork is a form of advocacy, in the sense that it is either advice directly concerned with the client's chances of success in proceedings, or the drafting of pleadings and other documents which are, in effect, written advocacy, and can have a significant effect on the ultimate outcome of any proceedings. At the end of the day, however, the barrister is judged on his ability in court.

This does not mean that the Bar is populated by actors manqués: whilst there are many areas of the Bar in which the colourful advocate still has his place, there is no doubt that the advocacy of the modern barrister is aimed at being effective rather than flamboyant. Effective advocacy means different things in different contexts; in criminal work it will involve remembering that the jury consists of ordinary people who are likely to be affected by common sense rather than purple passages. For a very large proportion of the Bar, now concerned with commercial work, it will involve the ability to analyse complex factual legal situations; and across the whole spectrum of the work the Bar does, there will always be the opportunity for the sort of intellectual debate which may be involved in taking a point of law through to the House of Lords. Advocacy does not mean simple oral advocacy. The Bar has always drafted the formal documents which go before the court, which may well be vital parts of the way in which a case is presented. Increasingly, evidence, and argument, are taken in written form by the courts: the barrister must therefore be persuasive on paper as well as on his feet. Of the 7,000 barristers who practice, about two-thirds do so from London, the remainder either from the main provincial centres in England and Wales, or in Europe. Barristers' chambers are an essential part of the way in which a barrister can work. Not only do they provide the accommodation and administration necessary for running a practice, but they are usually structured as a team providing essential support for one another, and a logical progression in career terms through from pupillage to pension, whether or not that includes a judicial appointment on the way.

Recruitment to chambers is nowadays dependent upon ability. The Bar recruits from across the spectrum of universities and polytechnics. At least one-third of those who are called to the Bar each year are women. Six per cent of the Bar come from ethnic minorities (a higher percentage than that of the ethnic minorities within the community). Those who describe it as elitist are correct, if by this they mean that the profession is one which is a meritocracy: they are wrong if by this they mean that it is now unrepresentative in terms of class, sex or race.

Legal executives
IAN WATSON

Ian Watson joined the Institute of Legal Executives after graduating with an honours degree in law. Currently the Secretary, Education and Training, he is well-placed to explain the role of this important legal body.

Legal executives are the modern descendants of solicitors' managing clerks – wily and experienced practitioners who long held a place in solicitors' offices. Starting out, literally, as clerks engrossing documents, years of patience and dedication imbued a detailed knowledge of clients' matters and legal procedures. However, with the passing of the quill pen and the arrival of typewriters, duplicators and the paraphernalia of the 'modern' office, the role of the clerk as a procedural expert developed and brought with it responsibility for matters undertaken on behalf of clients.

The legal executive's role

Now legal executives are important members of the team in most solicitors' practices, providing specialist support on procedural and legal matters. The role varies according to the structure of the office, but usually legal executives will be involved in one of the main practice specialisms such as conveyancing, criminal or civil litigation, matrimonial or probate and trusts work. A legal executive will often be responsible for the work of one or more of these specialist areas. Most legal executives are employed in solicitors' partnerships, but they are also found in industry, commerce and local and national government where there is a department dedicated to legal tasks.

So how does a legal executive differ from a solicitor? Mainly in two ways: status and qualification. Legal executives are employees. Solicitors' practices are constituted as partnerships and legal executives cannot become partners. They do not hold any rights of practice as such. These are limited by statute to solicitors or barristers and licensed conveyancers, or other authorized practitioners established under the Courts and Legal Services Act 1990. However, within the framework of private practice there are few practical limitations on the work which a legal executive can undertake. Client matters can normally be handled from start to finish; experienced legal executives may manage branch offices and sign cheques on their firms' clients accounts. In litigation matters, legal executives can appear before judges in chambers and, on certain uncontested matters, may appear in open court on behalf of their firm. However, there is no general right of audience in open court.

The other major difference between legal executives and solicitors is the mode of training. Nearly all solicitors now start their qualification by taking a degree, usually in law, sometimes in another subject, and follow this by a further one or two years' full-time study with the Law Society, before starting their practical experience in earnest in a solicitor's office. A trainee legal executive will start his, or increasingly her, practical training on day one, straight from school or following a change of career direction. They will gain practical experience and will support this by studying simultaneously for examinations set by the Institute of Legal Executives. The connection with the old managing clerks continues. The qualification of a legal executive is still firmly based in the practical world and experience is a vital component of it. However, to keep pace with modern requirements, it is essential to enhance experience by studying the substantive law and legal practice which the legal executive examinations cover.

The Institute of Legal Executives

The Institute of Legal Executives (ILEX) will be celebrating its 100th year in 1992. It was in 1892 that managing clerks perceived the value of banding together to contribute to their chosen profession and to promote their interests: 291 managing clerks met at the Girdler's Hall in London to inaugurate the Solicitors' Managing Clerks Association. The modern Institute was formed from the SMCA in 1963 with the support and cooperation of the Law Society. The aim was to provide a full training scheme and a career structure for solicitors' staff. The term managing clerk was, at that time, increasingly adopted and misused by employees who did not have sufficient experience. The term 'legal executive' was introduced so that employers would be able to identify those with experience and qualifications. The first group of legal executives was drawn from experienced managing clerks. However, the Institute's training scheme has become increasingly popular – in so far as examinations ever can be. The examination scheme was revised in 1982 to make it more appropriate to the needs of employers and to the needs of a much wider range of applicant. Approximately 3,000 new students enrol with the Institute each year and their qualifications and backgrounds range from youngsters with GCSE qualifications, through mature students with long clerical or secretarial experience in solicitors' offices, to law graduates, non-law graduates and mature entrants making a change of career. Over 17,000 subject entries were received for the main summer examination in 1991.

The training scheme

The training scheme now provides for study at two levels: Part I, roughly GCE A level standard, provides a broad introduction to all the major areas of law and legal practice likely to be encountered in a solicitors' practice or in a legal department. Part II is set at degree and professional standard and requires study of four subjects (three law, one practice) reflecting the area in which the particular student is specializing in his or her employment. To qualify fully as a Fellow, students must be twenty-five, and have at least five years' experience in legal practice, including at least two years after the examinations have been completed. Courses are offered at over a hundred colleges in England and Wales and the Institute has also established its own correspondence course service, ILEX Tutorial Services, which provides courses for all of the Institute's examinations and also for the examinations of the Law Society and London University.

The Institute also now offers an introductory qualification called the Preliminary Certificate in Legal Studies. It is aimed at prospective students who do not have the GCSE examinations needed to start the full examination scheme; and also at those who simply want a one-year introductory qualification in law and administration relevant to solicitors' work.

Membership

The Institute now has a membership of 21,500, principally in England and Wales, but with substantial branches in Hong Kong and Bermuda. Examinations are regularly taken in a number of Commonwealth countries where the legal system is still based on common law. The numbers of new students have increased steadily in recent years. Changes in patterns of qualification generally and the increased commitment of employers to education and training suggest that this trend will continue. The Institute publishes a monthly journal for members and provides the usual membership services. Its members are subject to a disciplinary code, in addition to the restrictions imposed by the Solicitors' Practice Rules.

Aims
The Institute is proud to be able to offer a career in the legal profession for those who have not, for whatever reason, been able to follow the standard routes to professional qualification. Its examinations have been recognized by the profession. Those who wish to extend their qualification and qualify as solicitors can gain exemption from the academic stage of the Law Society's training scheme by taking appropriate heads of the Institute's examination, and dispensation from articles is allowed to Fellows of the Institute. From 1993, the ILEX examinations will be the principal route recognized by the Law Society for non-graduates to qualify as solicitors. For those who wish to broaden their qualification by completing a degree, the University of London will grant exemption, head for head, from the Intermediate stage of the External LLB degree, and many polytechnics will give similar recognition in respect of their law degrees.

For the employer, the Institute's training scheme provides a valuable assurance that staff have acquired a grasp of a broad range of legal and procedural principles and a specialized knowledge of at least one area of legal practice and the law relating to it. The overall aim is to give staff working within the profession achievable career goals whilst enhancing and securing the quality of service provided to solicitors' clients.

Part II
The law degree

Why read law?
GARY SCANLAN

Gary Scanlan qualified as a Solicitor and is currently a Lecturer in Law at an English university. He has published numerous articles and reviews in professional legal journals and is the Consultant Editor of *The Legal Executive*. **He is the coauthor of** *An Introduction to Criminal Law,* **SWOT** *Criminal Law* **and** *A Guide to the Criminal Justice Act 1988,* **all published by Blackstone Press.**

This is the ultimate question for the budding law student, and is frequently put to such individuals when they are being interviewed for a place on a degree or professional law course.

The answers which are usually given exhibit certain attitudes which potential law students have, or at least profess to have, with regard to legal studies. Students sometimes state that they wish to study law because they want to help people. They may see themselves as future social reformers, using their dazzling legal skills to combat and correct society's ills. Others less exalted see the law as a meal ticket or as a status symbol, the thinking teenager's BMW. These professed reasons for reading law may have been fuelled by television, books, association with individuals involved in the law or experiences at school and work.

A student may subsequently find such reasons to be illusions. Society remains remarkably resilient to change, status is not what it was and a quick survey of salaries offered in the legal appointments pages of the 'quality' newspapers and professional journals shows that the path to riches for lawyers is narrow and full of pitfalls.

Despite realities, the seminal social reformers, status seekers and gold diggers may arrive at their law schools undiminished in the belief that their reasons for studying law are valid for their particular circumstances and these beliefs will sustain them through their student days and beyond.

Others may be less certain of their reasons for wanting to study law. They may wish to pursue a career as a barrister, legal executive or solicitor, or any of the professions or occupations for which a legal background may be a necessity, though they are not sure why they wish to pursue such a chosen career or to study law. The fact that a student may have no more than a 'gut' reaction that he/she feels that law studies are for him/her is as good a reason as any for undertaking such a course. At the cost of sounding pretentious or patronizing, young people embarking upon a chosen career do so frequently on the flimsiest of whims and rarely come to harm. Whether the course of studies chosen is the right one is impossible to determine and it is pointless to worry about what has already been undertaken. If the study of law is a mistake it is not a disaster, courses can be changed and what has been absorbed during a course of study is rarely without some value.

To sum up, the fact that you cannot rationalize and express in concrete terms your intention to study law does not mean that your desire to commence legal studies is ill-founded or that you would be unsuitable as a law student. The latter issue anyway can only be determined by embarking upon your legal studies.

If you decide to embark upon a law course take great care in selecting your law school. Write to the schools you are thinking of entering before you apply, asking whether they have open days and, if they do, make sure you attend one of them. If at all possible, when you visit a school make a special effort to talk to the resident students. It is an unfortunate fact of life that many law teachers do not take too great an interest in their students' studies (despite lip-service to the contrary); the nature of the teachers at your intended law schools can and should be ascertained by careful questioning of the 'customers'.

If you obtain a place at a law school in which you are left to your own devices this may not be a total disaster. Though a law school which has teachers who take an interest in a student's studies is desirable, you will find that the crucial element in your success as a law student is the effort you put into your studies. This is perhaps the principal reason to study law. Law is not only an academic discipline but a practical science. A student should from the very first day of his/her legal studies inculcate a sense of responsibility and maturity. He/she should show a sense of independence both of thought and expression. These qualities are in no way dependent upon any law teacher, who can only encourage their development; such qualities must be acquired by the student by his/her own endeavours.

Being a law student involves motivating yourself towards a carefully organized and structured approach to your legal studies. You must master the techniques of reading the many hundreds of reported decisions (or precedents) quickly and extracting from these cases the principles of law that constitute the common law, as well as coming to grips with the many Acts of Parliament which now regulate much of our law. The techniques involved in digesting these materials, which can only be acquired by trial and error, will provide you with the skills that are necessary to the successful professional, irrespective of the career you may undertake.

These skills and qualities involve the ability to digest large masses of material quickly and to apply only the knowledge gained which is relevant to a given situation. To be prepared to be flexible in the approach to the solving of problems is a key quality in any professional person; its cultivation must begin and can be developed at law school. The study of law, if approached in the right frame of mind, will help you to become a confident individual, capable of analysing complex problems, and able to express opinions on situations based upon rational thought and backed up by recourse to a source of relevant information obtained by diligent but effective and discriminating study.

In reality, most law students wish to use both the skills and qualities they have acquired and their knowledge of the law so that they may in future act as legal practitioners and advisers, and their study of law is devoted to this end. This is a laudable and worthwhile aim. The careers in the law that are open to you are discussed throughout the rest of this book and require little extra comment. The satisfaction that can arise from a legal career, irrespective of the prestige or wealth that can be derived, is enough to encourage many a young person to become a law student. Nevertheless, the study of law can in itself be a rewarding task without reference to a future career; you must not feel that law studies lead inexorably to a solicitor's office or barrister's chambers. First and foremost, a law student must commence his/her legal studies as an end in itself.

Finally, it must be said that you may find the study of law boring and lawyers insufferable: the latter is clearly understandable and almost certainly unavoidable; the former, happily for those who are young, is instantly remedied. To leave a law school and terminate your legal studies because you find that they are not for you should be as responsible and mature a decision as your decision to commence those studies, and, if based upon sound reasons, never to be regretted.

Swot English Legal System
2nd Edition   David Howarth   £8.95

Swot Employment Law
2nd Edition   Ann Holmes & Richard Painter   £8.95

Swot Commercial & Consumer Law
Graham Stephenson & Peter Clark   £8.95

Swot Revenue Law
Derek Martin   £8.95

Swot Jurisprudence
2nd Edition   Raymond Wacks   £8.95

Swot Company Law
3rd Edition   Allan Blake & Helen Bond   £8.95

Swot Law of Contract
4th Edition   Richard Taylor   £8.95

Swot Land Law
3rd Edition   Denise Artis & John Houghton   £8.95

Swot Criminal Law
3rd Edition   Christopher Ryan & Gary Scanlan   £8.95

Swot Family Law
3rd Edition   Duncan Bloy   £8.95

Swot Law of Evidence
2nd Edn. Christopher Carr & John Beaumont   £8.95

Swot Law of Torts
3rd Edition   Peter Clark & Graham Stephenson   £8.95

Swot Constitutional & Administrative Law
3rd Edition   Robert Lee   £8.95

Swot Equity & Trusts
3rd Edition   Paul Todd   £8.95

Swot A Level Law
2nd Edition   Nick Johnson & Alan Pannett   £8.95

Swot Conveyancing
Bridget Walker   £8.95

To be published in 1992: **Swot Succession**

 BLACKSTONE PRESS LIMITED
9-15 ALDINE STREET, LONDON W12 8AW Tel: 081 740 1173 Fax: 081 743 2292

Where to study law
BOB LEE

Bob Lee is Director of Research and Development at Wilde Sapte, one of the UK's largest firms of solicitors, based in the City of London, specializing in all aspects of commercial law. Prior to joining Wilde Sapte, Bob lectured in law in both a university and a polytechnic.

In spite of the recession and a general slow-down in work for lawyers, there is no shortage of candidates applying for training contracts. This seems wise. The recession will not last indefinitely, and the prognosis for the 1990s should remain healthy with the growth of the European single market, the internationalization of legal work, and the relentless growth in regulation of social and economic activity. At the moment, however, it is tougher than it has been for some years to find a place in a law firm. So how do you choose a degree course in law that will place you ahead of the field?

To some extent, the answer to this question is dictated by your A level examination results. These may rule out a degree in law altogether, if so do not despair. Many firms now take up to half of their trainees from non-law degree courses. Equally, your A level grades may confine you to an institution which makes a lower level of offer, and these tend to be polytechnics. However, simply because the institution offers lower grades it does not follow that the quality of educational provision is poorer. Their intake may have low grades, but their output may be high in achievement. Bear in mind that A level averages may remain low because student choice is relatively uninformed, so that factors such as geographical location may prove more decisive than course content or teaching method in making choices. But let us assume for a moment that all of your examinations are graded at the highest possible level, so that you have a free choice of institution – where do you choose?

Oxbridge?

If this is so, you have to begin by looking at Oxford and Cambridge Universities. There are a number of reasons for saying this. At least for your initial posting following graduation, there are some strategic advantages to being an Oxbridge graduate. Almost irrespective of degree level, it is easier to acquire job offers. Indeed, the notion of finals, with all examinations relevant to degree classification at the end of the third year, makes it more difficult to predict what degree the Oxbridge undergraduate will obtain. But this does not prove a barrier to finding work. In addition, you will be taught by well-respected, and often famous, academics. Moreover, both are attractive towns in which to be a student, but remember that we said that course content and teaching method might be more important than location.

The teaching method is certainly rather different. You will be taught primarily by tutors from your college. They will take you for intensive tutorial work which will be based on assignments which you have prepared, and in responding to these your tutor may offer what amounts to a cross between personal tuition and medieval torture. Lectures are held on a university rather than college basis, and attendance, which is optional, may vary considerably depending on the quality of the lecturer. Although the notion of tutoring in this way may seem designed to fit your individual needs, the reality may on occasions be different. Tutors may cover a wide range of subjects, and the tuition may lack the excitement of the more inventive, group-based work of new institutions.

University or polytechnic?

So, Oxbridge is an attractive choice but by no means an automatic one, and, if you are not a self-confident individual, you may feel better suited elsewhere. Presumably you look at universities next and, if that fails, polytechnics? Although this is a pattern which many candidates follow, it is not obviously correct. Polytechnics are the first choice for some students because they offer more flexibility of access and tuition. As such they appeal to mature students, for example. They may provide more guidance through the law degree, and pay greater pastoral attention to students. The lecturers may place more emphasis on the teaching element within their job, and may have received a better grounding in educational theory. On the other hand, universities are better resourced for the most part. This may affect the quality of your course, via library provision for example, but it may affect, also, the quality of your student life in terms of accommodation, sports facilities and the like.

These are huge generalizations, and institutions vary across what is called the 'binary divide'. Some polytechnic law schools are ahead of some universities in the quality of their legal education – but some are not. So do you apply to university or polytechnic? The answer is simple. Apply to both. Read the prospectus for each chosen institution carefully, attempt to visit the place, and try to decide where it is that you will be happy. Three years is a long time to spend in a place which you dislike, and even the fact that it has the top four law professors in the country may not cheer you up very much.

There have been career advantages traditionally in attending a university. However, the Government are committed to abolishing the distinction between universities and polytechnics. All will become universities. For a time some note may be made as to the history and background of the institution. But as times goes by, and as recruitment gets tougher, employers will look to the current quality of the institution whatever its former status. In any case, once in a job, future employers tend to be more interested in what you achieved in that job than where you studied for your degree.

Type of degree

One note of caution: do not imagine that all law degrees are the same. The variety of approaches to the academic stage of legal training are enormous. There are three main camps, however, and it is as well to be aware of these. The first is the traditional pattern of law teaching – sometimes labelled 'black letter' law. This name is intended to imply that the course will not look at many sources beyond law. It will concentrate on law as found in the law reports and statutes, attempting to trace the legal rules or doctrines which flow from these sources. It can be contrasted with the more 'contextual' approach. This name hints that it may be necessary to look at law in its economic, social or political contexts, so that review will not focus on a narrow range of legal sources. Finally, there exists a more theoretical approach, increasingly based in 'critical' legal theory, and heavily dominated by a rapidly burgeoning literature on the role of law in modern society.

Now, you cannot be expected to understand these different approaches fully in advance of meeting them, but I do recommend that you attempt to trace the nature of the degree courses for which you apply, because you may relish or hate the prospect of an approach to law which has a heavily philosophical bent. Moreover, the picture is not as clear as I have made out. Comparatively few law schools would advertise themselves as committed to one of the above approaches. Indeed there may be no uniform view within the law school as to which should prevail. So read the prospectus carefully and try and ascertain the nature of the discipline you are actually being asked to study in your 'law' degree.

As to which is best in career terms, the answer may be that there is no one winner. 'Black letter' law may appear to be more relevant, but it may bear little actual resemblance to the work which you will do in practice. On the other hand 'black letter' lawyers would argue that other approaches place too little emphasis on core legal concepts. Remember that the law degree is only the first stage of training for a career in law. A year of study for professional examinations plus periods in articles or pupillage will follow. The best advice is to choose a course which appeals to you. You are likely to succeed at something if you are interested in it. Good luck!

Preparation for the course
CHRISTOPHER RYAN

Christopher Ryan is a Senior Lecturer in Law in the Department of Law at City University. He has taught law at a university in New Zealand and also at Liverpool University, Kingston-upon-Thames Polytechnic, and Buckingham University. He is author and coauthor of several books on criminal law and company law, and he is also chief examiner for the regulation and compliance paper of the Securities Industry examination under the auspices of The Stock Exchange. He has wide experience of advising students.

If you are embarking upon any course in law this does not necessarily mean that you will finish up in practice as a barrister, solicitor or legal executive. It is still true that the majority of students who set out to obtain a law degree or professional qualification in law do intend to make careers as practising lawyers, but a law degree is an appropriate qualification and as acceptable as an arts or science degree for careers in commerce or industry (as executives, managers, public relations and personnel officers), the civil service, police, military, local government administration, court administration or accountancy. Secondly, if you are thinking about or have made a decision to study law you should know that it will require dedication, application and persistent industry on your part. The study of law requires you to read a vast amount of reported cases as well as commentaries on the law. This necessitates development of such skills as rapid comprehension and the ability to assimilate only material that is strictly relevant, to analyse it and argue by analogy from that material. This means that, preferably, you should come equipped with the powers of concentration of a surgeon, the commitment of a monastic, and the agility of mind and logicality of a chess grand master. You will get by with lesser endowments or attributes of skill but only through hard work.

The best preparation, therefore, for so rigorous a course is making absolutely certain you know what you are setting out to achieve and why. Only if you are certain that law is the course for you will you be well prepared to do battle with it. To be certain, you need to inform yourself about the course, the legal professions and alternative careers. You need to query why you are enrolling for a law course. If you are someone who is simply following in your father's footsteps or who has been 'pushed' by the upwardly mobile aspirations of parents or by careers teachers, who realize you will not quite make the grade for the medical profession, you are not a student 'well prepared' to study law. In order to test your certainty, but also as preparation, you should at the earliest opportunity apply to a local solicitor and/or to the head of a barrister's chambers for permission to spend a week in the office or chambers observing and asking questions. You should also visit court hearings. Our courts are in the main open to the public. You will not always understand what is going on but the familiarity and the 'feel' that you get from being an observer in local magistrates', county, crown and high courts can be very useful in the early stage of a law course. Do not be shy. Good lawyers need initiative and a touch of audacity, therefore you should try and organize a visit to a solicitor's office and to a barrister's chambers yourself by presenting them with your request in writing. Solicitors' firms are well advertised in telephone directories or on windows in the high street, but the local law society or the Law Society (113 Chancery Lane, London WC2A 1PL. Tel: 071-242 1222) would provide you with the names of firms in your area. Barristers are not so easy to find because they do not have direct contact with the public, but a solicitor or, again, the Law Society, would provide you with the names to contact, or an enquiry could be made to The General Council of the Bar (11 South Square, Gray's Inn, London WC1R 5EL. Tel: 071-242 0082). While the thought of visiting courts may seem daunting it need not be in reality because they are staffed by porters, ushers and court clerks all of whom, provided you are polite and presentable, will be very willing to assist you.

Apart from being certain that you really want to study law, and apart from some degree of familiarity with the process of justice conducted in the courts and the role and world of legal practitioners, there is no crucial preparation prior to the start of the degree course. Many students are advised or think they need to study A level law as a precondition. If you think it will help you make up your mind then go ahead but it is *not* necessary: in fact many law lecturers at degree level would prefer that you had not done so on the basis that a little law learning is a dangerous thing, particularly if such courses simply get you into the habit of rote learning and regurgitation. Most degree courses either have induction courses in the first few weeks or else are designed to ease you into the study of law, so that no A level or other preliminary law course is necessary prior to starting at university or polytechnic.

Familiarity with legal terminology is a useful prerequisite and there are certain oft-recommended books of a general nature which serve that purpose as well as illuminating in a simple way what the legal system, the study and the practice of law are all about. It would help if you read the following before the course starts: Glanville Williams, *Learning the Law* (11th ed. 1982), Stevens, and/or A W B Simpson, *Invitation to Law* (1988) Blackwell. Otherwise choose from: R White, *The Administration of Justice* (1985), Basil Blackwell; P Atiyah, *Law and Modern Society* (1963), Oxford University Press; or R Rubinstein, *John Citizen and the Law*, Penguin Books; J P Derriman, *Discovering the Law*, University of London Press; J Malcolm, *Let's Make it Legal*, Education Explorers.

In relation to legal careers, see B Hogan, *A Career in Law* (1981), Sweet & Maxwell, or R Miller and A Alston, *Equal Opportunities: A Career Guide* (1984), Penguin.

In so far as preparing for the mechanics of study are concerned some help may be obtained from: Bradney, Fisher, Masson, Neal and Newell, *How to Study Law* (1986), Sweet & Maxwell; J Dane and P Thomas, *How to Use a Law Library* (2nd ed. 1985), Sweet & Maxwell; and in particular the first two chapters of any of the SWOT series of study aid books published by Blackstone Press, eg Chapters 1 and 2 of Ryan and Scanlan, *SWOT Criminal Law* (3rd ed. 1991), Chapters 1 and 2 of Taylor's *SWOT Law of Contract* (4th ed. 1992).

Finally, a law student and a lawyer in practice has to be articulate and skilful with words, therefore participation in debating is good preparation, as is being well read both in the classics of English literature and in English history, especially those aspects relating to the development of our constitution.

To sum up, certainty that the course is right for you, general familiarity with the purpose of law, the legal system, and its personnel and terminology are good enough preparation. However, that preparation together with a developed fortitude to ask questions, a polished eloquence and some pretested ability to discipline yourself to a regular, unsupervised work schedule would provide an even more useful preparation for a degree course in law.

Part III
Becoming a solicitor

Routes into the profession
RICHARD RAMSAY

There are several ways in which one may become a solicitor. Richard Ramsay, a Barrister who is a Director of Cadmus Legal Education, a company providing continuing education for the legal profession, discusses these below. The present demand for newly qualified solicitors remains high and shows little sign of abating. Perhaps it all goes to show the truth of the old story about the lone lawyer in the small American town who could get no work at all. When a second lawyer arrived they were both very busy!

'Of the making of lawyers there is no end', Francis Bacon might have said and, of those lawyers, the majority will be solicitors. It is, however, more difficult to say exactly what a typical solicitor does and, in reality, it is impossible to give a simple answer. Many work in the public sector, or in industry and commerce, but the majority are in private practice. Some of these are in 'high street' practices, perhaps sole practitioners or in small firms. Others are in larger firms, possibly in the City, where one alone has some two hundred partners.

Whatever their work, solicitors will have four elements in their education: an academic stage, a vocational stage, a professional stage and continuing education. Little needs to be said about the first part as the subject of law degrees is dealt with elsewhere in this publication. It is, however, worth stressing that, whilst solicitors, like most other professions, have moved to effectively all-graduate recruitment this does not mean that all entrants are law graduates, or that all solicitors, let alone all those recently admitted, are graduates at all.

The academic stage

For law graduates the matter is relatively simple. As soon as they have completed their law degrees they are eligible to pass on to the next stage. This assumes that they have covered the six 'core' subjects (constitutional law, contract, tort, criminal law, land law and trusts) during their studies but this is almost certain to be the case as they are normally compulsory components. Not all law graduates go on to take the Solicitors' Finals examination or any other professional qualification but the benefit of doing so is considerable.

For the non-law graduate the matter is rather less straightforward in that they must study for a further year on an intensive course, the Common Professional Examination, which involves taking all the 'core' subjects. This can be a more difficult route because the content of the course is very demanding: it takes a full year rather than the traditional academic year. Moreover, it is unlikely that the graduate will be publicly financed once he or she has completed a first degree. Discretionary grants are increasingly difficult to obtain but private support may be available. The course may be undertaken at the College of Law or at one of a number of polytechnics. Intending candidates should realize that, whereas the law degree opens doors to both the Bar and the solicitors' profession, the academic stage is, despite its name, not truly common to both in that different establishments prepare students for the different branches.

In theory, mature students may spend two years on the Common Professional Examination course and take eight subjects, though it is difficult to find places where this option can be undertaken. They might therefore find a part-time course leading to a law degree an attractive alternative. The law is not a career where age is necessarily a barrier. Well over half of the practising solicitors in this country are under forty and partnerships can be achieved by people in their mid-thirties – sometimes earlier – but maturity can be as important a quality as dynamic youthfulness. There is no doubt, however, that the profession is getting younger, as any perusal of the faces of new partners in a weekly journal such as *The Lawyer* will show.

It is also fair to add here that as many women as men are now being admitted as solicitors and many are encouraged to return to their career after having babies – several City firms now organize creches and perhaps the Law Society should consider the possibility of articles being served in the cradle! A year ago it seemed that there was apparently an ever-open demand for new solicitors and this showed no prospect in the foreseeable future of drying up. One cannot afford to be so sanguine now. There are not only redundancies in conveyancing departments but several firms are cutting back on the recruitment of trainee solicitors. Trainees may increasingly find that there is no vacancy for them after they have completed their training. There is less corporate merger and acquisition work but insolvency is on the increase. The need is still greatest in the company and commercial areas. Good new graduates are still much sought after. There is, however, competition for places in the best firms and it should be remembered that offers are made for entry into the firm some two years later. Less well-qualified graduates may find considerable problems in obtaining a vacancy for traineeship as well as a permanent post.

The vocational stage

To have to think about one's career during the academic stage of one's education may seem a little sudden, but forward planning is necessary. Places for the vocational stage can be swallowed up rapidly and at one time there seemed to be something approaching a trade in places at the College of Law. In 1990 a further college at York opened, in addition to those at Guildford, Chester and London. Students may be as well to go to a polytechnic for their Solicitors' Finals – especially if it is near their home – as the basis of the course is a set of materials supplied by the Law Society which are then fleshed out by one's lecturers.

The Finals course is intensive and there are heavy demands on the student's time and concentration during the year. There is a great deal of material and much of it must be committed to memory. Changes are now in the offing, however, as skills training becomes more important than straightforward 'black letter' law. Attempts are made to ensure that the examinations are relevant to practice but students may find that they cover subjects which they neither wish nor will be required to use in practice. The Finals course is intended to provide a transitional phase between academic life and the world of work. It is helpful to have a common sense approach to learning at this point.

For the moment the foregoing is true but the present pattern of Finals courses will end in June 1993. After that, various establishments – it is still not known which will be successful – will offer their own internally validated courses. This represents a significant development but it is very much in the melting pot at the time of writing. The fees are likely to increase from approximately £3,000 to £4,500 and this may cause especial hardship in an economic climate where students are less likely to obtain the necessary local authority discretionary grant or sponsorship funding. A professional studies loan may be the only recourse. Perhaps it is worth recalling that the ancient admonition, 'May you live in exciting times' was seen more as a curse than a blessing. A possible benefit is the likelihood of distance learning.

The professional stage

Where articles are served may determine the whole direction of one's later practice. It is usually possible to spend some time with a firm during a period of 'mini-articles' during a long vacation and this provides a good opportunity for the firm to make a better assessment of students' abilities should they wish to apply later. This is a very effective way for firms to recruit the best people by observing them over a period of time early on. If they are very impressed they may go as far as offering some financial incentives, such as payment towards fees and maintenance during the Solicitors' Finals year. It is possible for students to assess the firm as well, to see if it is the kind of environment in which they feel comfortable. Many firms trawl in universities and polytechnics to attract the best students but if a particular establishment is not on the 'milk round' there is nothing to stop individuals from contacting the firms which interest them directly. Student issues of *The Lawyer* are very useful as a source of information about specific firms and most now publish an elegant brochure for recruitment purposes.

It is up to the individual to arrange articles, but the Law Society has a Register of Solicitors Employing Trainees (ROSET), of which there should be copies in universities and polytechnics. It is always worth seeking the help of the appointments board at educational establishments for general advice.

It cannot be stressed too much that students should look around carefully before making a decision and be prepared for a long search for a post. Although the period of articles means that trainee solicitors will be required to experience a number of aspects of the solicitor's work, what the firm does depends very much on what the firm is.

Continuing education

Although a barrister is called to the Bar after passing the relevant examinations and eating the relevant number of dinners, solicitors are only admitted to the Roll after they have satisfactorily completed their period of articles. Even this is not entirely the end, for solicitors must now attend a number of courses in their first three years of post-qualification experience. This requirement now extends to the rest of their practising lives (the Bar has, for reasons better known to itself, been very reluctant to extend the concept of continuing education to its members). A few people think of this as a chore but for the vast majority it is a valuable means of developing their knowledge and keeping up to date with the fast moving world of the law today.

The larger firms tend to have a training or education director specifically in charge of trainee solicitors and continuing education. Sometimes they double this with responsibility for recruitment. Other firms delegate these tasks to a partner. The quality of post-qualification education and training may well be a major element in the decision to join one firm or another these days. The continuing education requirement may be satisfied by going on courses provided by public or private trainers (all of them must be approved) but a larger firm is likely to undertake at least some of its training commitment 'in-house'.

The necessary qualities

The Law Society publishes a useful document, *Solicitors – A Career for Tomorrow*, obtainable from the Law Society shop, 227 Strand, London WC2R 1BA. Tel: 071-242 1222. This lists the desirable academic qualities as: a good memory, numeracy, a good command of language and the ability to get to grips with a problem. Personal attributes include integrity, the ability to communicate effectively, patience, and coolness under pressure. All those interested in becoming solicitors should obtain this publication, which is enlivened by a number of personal career profiles.

In summary, then, the majority of solicitors will now be law graduates, with some non-law graduates who have decided to 'convert' after their first degree. Some will be mature entrants – for the person over twenty-five already working in a law firm, perhaps in a secretarial capacity, this can be a very realistic route and several training directors are alert to the need to 'talent spot' among the ancillary staff of their firms. The only effective way for a non-graduate to become a solicitor will be by first qualifying as a Legal Executive.

Finally, there are transfers from members of the Bar, who are required to pass a single examination in professional ethics and accounts, but barristers who contemplate a change may work in a solicitor's office for a period before re-qualifying. Re-qualification for experienced barristers is now much easier. Such a step is obviously desirable for those who wish to reach the pinnacle of the solicitor in private practice – to become an equity partner. Although this may be seen as a 'back door route', the Law Society has decided not to close it.

In the present climate of many open opportunities it is almost superfluous to wish the eager candidate, 'Good Luck!' although the path is not entirely without difficulties.

The formal training and examinations
COLIN BEATTY

Colin Beatty is the Senior Policy Executive for Legal Education and Training at the Law Society.

Before a person may give notice for admission as a solicitor he must have completed three stages of training: the academic stage, the vocational stage and the practical stage. Normally the academic stage and vocational stage are completed before the practical stage which is met by serving under articles of training for a period of two years. The academic stage is usually met in one of three ways: by graduating with a qualifying law degree, by passing or being granted exemption from a Common Professional Examination (CPE) or by the award of a postgraduate diploma in law. The vocational stage is met by attending a one-year full-time or a two-year part-time Legal Practice Course and passing the assessments set during the course.

The academic stage of training

The academic stage of training required to be completed by those wishing to gain admission as solicitor may be met in one of three ways.

The qualifying law degree

The award of a qualifying law degree at a university or polytechnic in England and Wales, in which a student has studied and passed the assessments in the six core subjects of constitutional and administrative law; contract; torts; criminal law; land law; and equity and trusts, is held to complete the academic stage of training. Failure to pass the assessments in each of the six core subjects will result in a student spending an additional year studying any outstanding core subject or subjects and passing a paper or papers in a Common Professional Examination.

The Common Professional Examination

Graduates holding a degree awarded at a university or polytechnic in the United Kingdom or at an overseas university recognized by the Law Society, complete the academic stage of training by passing a Common Professional Examination, comprising the six core subjects: constitutional and administrative law; contract; torts; criminal law; land law; and equity and trusts. Students who have passed three or more corresponding law subjects within degree studies, and that degree has been awarded, may claim exemption from three or more of the papers set in the CPE. Students who have passed one or two corresponding law papers within degree studies are required to pass the full examination of six subjects.

The postgraduate diploma in law

Graduates may also complete the academic stage of training by the award of a postgraduate diploma in law, at a university or polytechnic which has included a study of the six core subjects and is recognized by the Law Society.

It is possible to obtain each of these qualifications by part-time study but a student studying for a part-time law degree must complete his studies in not more than six years and a student studying for a part-time CPE or a part-time postgraduate diploma in law must complete his studies in not more than two years.

Fellows of the Institute of Legal Executives

A fellow of the Institute of Legal Executives may claim exemption from the Common Professional Examination by virtue of passing the corresponding six papers in the Institute of Legal Executives Part II examinations. This now constitutes the only route by which non-graduates may qualify as solicitors.

The vocational stage of training

In May 1990, the Council of the Law Society approved in principle the Training Committee's report 'Training Tomorrow's Solicitors'. The report proposed that the Law Society's Final Course and Final Examination for solicitors should be replaced in September 1993 by a more practical Legal Practice Course. The Legal Practice Course will be taught and assessed by approved institutions subject to the Society's supervision.

The purpose of the Legal Practice Course is to ensure that trainee solicitors entering training contracts have the necessary knowledge and skills to undertake appropriate tasks under proper supervision during the contract. A full-time Legal Practice Course will run for one academic year; a part-time Legal Practice Course will run for two years. The introduction of part-time courses will increase the flexibility of the Law Society's training scheme and access to the profession.

The curriculum of the Legal Practice Course comprises:
(a) *Compulsory areas*. Conveyancing; wills, probate and administration; business law and practice; litigation and advocacy. All four of these compulsory areas will combine substantive law, procedure and practical skills work.
 b) *Optional subjects*. Students will be required to study two optional courses from a range of subjects of interest in 'private client' and 'corporate client' work.
(c) *Pervasive topics*. Certain topics have been identified as of such importance that they should be assessed through the compulsory areas. These topics include: professional ethics and conduct; investment business under the Financial Services Act; European Community law; revenue law.
(d) *Practical skills*. The Legal Practice Course will seek to develop certain essential skills including: practical legal research; drafting; interviewing; negotiating and advocacy.
(e) *Assessment*. Assessment of the Legal Practice Course will be the responsibility of the teaching institutions. It will comprise a mixture of written examinations, coursework and the assessment of skills.

Application for places on the Legal Practice Course are made to the Central Applications Board, Admail 44, London SW1P 1YL. Application forms should be obtained from the Board and should be completed and returned to the Board not later than 31st December of the year before you wish to commence the LPC.

The practical stage of training

The practical stage of training is met by serving a two-year training contract under the supervision of a solicitor qualified and practising in England and Wales and successfully completing a Professional Skills Course.

During the training contract the trainee solicitor will put into practice the skills and knowledge he has gained while completing the academic and vocational stages of training. A trainee solicitor will normally occupy three seats, each in a different area of legal practice, he will also gain a knowledge of office practice and procedures.

The aim of the Professional Skills Course is to build on the foundations laid in the Legal Practice Course and to ensure that all trainee solicitors during the training contract period receive formal instruction in those practical matters which assume some understanding of how legal offices operate.

The areas covered will be: accounts; investment business; professional work management; professional conduct; advocacy. All trainee solicitors will have to complete all sections of the Professional Skills Course satisfactorily before being admitted as solicitors.

Continuing education

The education and training of solicitors does not end on admission to the Roll. All persons admitted as solicitors after August 1987 are required to undertake continuing education as long as they remain in practice.

(a) The Professional Development Course. This course is a one-day compulsory course taken in a solicitor's first year after admission. The course comes into effect in January 1992 and will replace the 'Category A' years 1 and 2 courses. The course will be organized by approved providers designated by the Law Society.

(b) 'Best Practice'. It is now compulsory for all newly admitted solicitors to take a management training course approved by the Law Society and based on the 'Best Practice' management training kit. The course lasts for a minimum of one day and must be taken in the third year after admission.

(c) Extension of the continuing education scheme to the whole profession. The Council have agreed in principle that the continuing education scheme should be extended to the whole profession. Although the Strategy Committee has suggested that all those admitted since 1965 should be brought within the scheme by 1995, no decisions on the timetable for extending the scheme have yet been taken.

Proposals to extend the scheme further will be considered by the Law Society during the first half of 1992. The proposals will canvass the way in which continuing education can best address the needs of more experienced practitioners, for example, by providing more high level courses, more distance learning courses and by giving extra continuing education points to solicitors involved in presenting courses. The Society is also considering ways in which the scheme can be streamlined.

Training within a large firm
TOM PURTON

Tom Purton joined Freshfields, a large City law firm, as a trainee solicitor in September 1988. He now works in the company department at Freshfields having spent six months in their New York office.

Training within a large firm extends well beyond technical knowledge. It is characterized by 'on-the-job' training and complemented by a formal programme designed to supplement and accelerate the process of practical learning. The purpose of this article is to provide an overview of that training and, in particular, to identify to what extent it differs from training in a smaller organization.

Formal training programme

This falls into three main categories; induction, technical training and skills training.

Induction: Most large firms run an induction course designed to introduce the new recruit to the organization and administration of the firm. There are generally two parts: one covering the firm as a whole and a second dealing with each department. Another element of the induction programme is a series of lectures organized by seven of the largest City firms and given by City practitioners. This is designed to provide an understanding of the City and to put into a business context the law and transactions dealt with by larger firms. At Freshfields, there are also a series of newcomers' seminars covering a variety of technical topics.

Technical training: This explains the legal framework for a variety of transactions and why they are structured in a particular way. It is designed to improve not only your knowledge of substantive law but to put that knowledge into context. Thus, it includes case studies involving drafting documents and identifying the legal issues which need to be addressed. It is particularly useful because it provides an overview of different transactions from beginning to end without the pressure and time constraints invariably associated with a 'live' transaction.

Skills training: Skills training covers areas which, historically, were learnt entirely through experience such as researching, negotiating, legal drafting and general interpersonal skills. Whilst the practical on-the-job training is geared to develop such skills, the formal programme provides a framework within which to nurture them. It also includes information technology such as training on computers, in-house information systems and Lexis, the computer legal reference data base. Language courses for all levels of expertise are an optional extra.

On-the-job training

Training at Freshfields begins in one of three departments – company, litigation or property. Shortly after joining the firm, you are invited to discuss your particular interests with the recruitment training partner who structures your progress through the different departments (subject to the regulations that require all firms to provide you with experience of at least three main practice areas). This training pattern is not, however, written in stone and can be negotiated if you have a change of heart.

You are generally in each department for six months and always share a room with a qualified lawyer (in some firms, with a partner). The work you undertake includes researching points of law, drafting documents and letters of advice and attending meetings. Each department has a partner with specific responsibility for training. This partner reviews the nature of the work each trainee has done at regular intervals and tries to ensure a varied work load. The transition from academic law to general practice is slow and often difficult. It is not realistic to expect to manage a complex transaction without close supervision and guidance. At times, this is harsh medicine to swallow. After law finals, you reach the end of a lengthy stage of academic training, only to find yourself at the beginning of another training process on joining a law firm. The difference, however, is that finally you are putting theory into practice (and getting paid for it!).

A trainee has a number of roles to play. As a junior member of a team, you cannot always be guaranteed interesting work. What is certain is that by being involved in a transaction and supervised where necessary in the work you undertake, you learn how to manage a transaction more effectively. When you come to do a similar deal, you are therefore better placed to handle it. In a large firm there are a great number of people with varied experience and expertise in different areas of law. There are also impressive service departments such as the library, information bank (containing memoranda, practice notes and other technical information in all areas of law undertaken by the firm), 24 hour word processing, photocopying etc. The advantage for a trainee is two-fold. First, there is invariably someone with experience in an area which you have been asked to assist on. In my experience, most people are only too happy to point you in the right direction. Second, the support departments are designed to make the lives of all lawyers in the firm easier whether they be a trainee or a partner. It allows you to concentrate on your legal work and avoids junior members of the firm (ie trainees) spending hours mastering the art of photocopying!

Large firms tend to handle complex transactions. As your knowledge of a type of transaction and the law relating to it develops, so does the extent to which you can assume responsibility and increase your exposure to clients. It is counterproductive both for the trainee and the firm to overburden a new recruit. In a large firm, you are encouraged to take an increasing amount of responsibility as the training period progresses. However, no client (quite rightly) wishes to deal with an inexperienced lawyer who inevitably has to refer constantly to someone more senior. It is, at times, frustrating but is an unavoidable part of the learning curve.

It is often said that joining a large firm carries with it the danger of joining an impersonal organization. An additional concern is that a trainee's level of responsibility and exposure to clients is far more limited than in a small firm. There is some truth in both comments. There is little doubt that joining a firm with over twelve hundred employees worldwide is somewhat daunting. However, by necessity, a trainee works with a relatively small group of people in every department. For example, the company department at Freshfields (which is by far the largest) is divided into six teams all of which cover three areas of specialization. Each team contains between twenty-five and thirty people. That group of people operate as a unit which has all the intimacy associated with a small firm but carries the advantage of having a vast array of both legal and administrative support to rely on when necessary.

On the sport and social side, large firms provide an impressive range of events. At Freshfields, cricket, football, rugby, hockey, squash and tennis are just a selection of the activities organized. There is even a gym in the building. You are part of a large group of young people most of whom are only too willing to indulge in social events. There is a great sense of identity in an environment like this and a ready-made social life is there as and when you want it.

An opportunity to work abroad is also a possibility towards the end of your training. Most large firms have extensive foreign offices. At Freshfields, twenty-four trainees each year spend time in either New York, Hong Kong, Singapore, Paris, Tokyo, Brussels, Frankfurt or Madrid. My six months in New York provided invaluable exposure to a different working culture.

In the past, a structured training programme (particularly technical and skills training) was unknown. It was assumed that a trainee would learn the art of a practitioner by a process of osmosis. Extensive resources and manpower are now devoted to training. A brief glimpse of a brochure for any major City firm will convince you of that. The quality of that training relies on a structured blend of formal instruction and constant involvement in real work. Like most important decisions, choosing which type of firm to join is not easy. Nor does one type of firm suit everyone. A large firm offers prestige, quality work, extensive resources and an opportunity to travel. Above all, it provides an excellent platform for a rewarding career.

Articles within the smaller firm
PAUL TRIM

Paul Trim was admitted in 1973 and is a Partner in Taylor Willcocks, a five-partner practice with four offices across South London and North Surrey. He joined the firm twelve years ago after serving articles and working for some years in Central London.

As a result of the nature of the Law Society's training course, it is probably easier today than it has ever been to achieve a perspective of the legal profession and its constituent parts before making that crucial decision as to where to set about applying for articles.

Changes in the profession

A few years ago there was a much greater overlap in the spheres of work of larger firms, in the City of London and Inns of Court areas for example, and provincial practices in both the suburbs and in the country. Financial constraints have changed this to the extent that many City practices now involve themselves hardly at all in private client work, so that City training may mean that the trainee sees little or nothing of the more personal aspects of solicitor-client relationships, which are the essence of general practice.

Conversely, many smaller firms have involved themselves much more in commercial work of recent years, so that, a well-balanced provincial practice may be able to offer prospective trainees a much greater scope for all-round experience than the large City outfit.

Part of the reason for all of this is the change which has come about in the requirements of the public from the legal profession, more and more complexities and pitfalls in the commercial world, coupled with a complete change in the nature of conveyancing practice, traditionally the profession's bread and butter.

Choice of practice

It is, of course, important for any trainee to consider carefully the nature and types of work undertaken by the firm which he or she contemplates joining, and to make enquiries to ensure that the scope is available for involvement in as many areas of practice as possible. Provided, however, that sufficient scope exists, there are without doubt very considerable benefits in this type of training.

One of the great advantages which the solicitor has as general practitioner, is the ability to interrelate different areas of law due to his or her 'across-the-board' knowledge, as opposed to the 'straight-jacketed' approach necessarily taken by some of those restrictively qualified in one field or another, such as licenced conveyancers.

The public, as a whole, is still appreciative of this ability and I believe that for the future it will become more not less important in an increasingly impersonal world.

Variety

Smaller practices have the ability to afford variety of experience to enable the trainee solicitor to achieve all-roundedness and be able, at the end of the day, to make a more reasoned choice as to what particular field he or she wishes to be involved in in the long term.

It should be remembered that there may be a considerable diversity of specialization in a smaller practice because frequently the partners have come from very different training backgrounds, from large City firms to provincial local authorities for example.

Students will understand that there is a world of difference between the corporate and private client work, and the personal contacts which are afforded by the smaller firm in the latter provide invaluable experience in the long run.

Advantages

Many larger firms have a fairly rigid approach to their training programmes – an organizational necessity in many cases – so that students spend a limited time, say six months, in one department, from which they then detach themselves completely and move to another. Whilst this clearly enables a trainee to see 'what goes on' in all the various sections of the firm, it has one major disadvantage. That is that it lacks the ability for the trainee to see a matter through from start to finish and so share in the satisfaction of achieving a result and, hopefully, a contented client.

There are comparatively few matters of any weight which begin and end within a six month period and because of the greater flexibility within a smaller firm, the trainee will have the ability to overlap different types of work, if appropriate, and have the experience of conducting a matter be it contentious or noncontentious, from beginning to end.

Career advisers are increasingly aware of the good training to be found in smaller and provincial firms and the Law Society's Training Committee are taking active steps to bolster the network of practices across the country which provide such training. The majority of practising solicitors are probably best described as general practitioners and enjoy the variety of work which that role entails.

For the student not wishing to end up as a commercial specialist therefore, there are very considerable advantages in choosing the smaller rather than the larger practice as a training forum.

Notes on qualifying as a solicitor

General

(a) Law graduates do the one-year Legal Practice Course (LPC).
(b) Non-law graduates must first pass the Common Professional Examination (CPE) or a postgraduate diploma in law.
(c) After passing the LPC you serve two years' articles, usually with a firm of solicitors but perhaps in local government, industry or a law centre and must pass a Professional Skills Course.
(d) Finally, you are admitted to the Roll of Solicitors.

The Common Professional Examination

(a) This one-year course teaches non-law graduates enough basic law to enable them to go on the LPC.
(b) CPE courses take place at the College of Law and at various polytechnics and universities.
(c) Places on CPE courses are in short supply. Apply in time.
(d) Your careers service has application forms and dates.
(e) Obtain a Certificate of Eligibility, from the Law Society. A certificate will not be issued until you have been awarded your degree and have a provisional offer of a place on a CPE course.
(f) Check to see whether your degree exempts you from any papers but note the CPE Board will not grant exemption from less than three core subjects of the Common Professional Examination. A student who has passed one or two corresponding law papers in degree studies is required to take the full CPE of six subjects.
(g) The papers cover contract, tort, criminal law, land law, equity and trusts, and constitutional and administrative law.
(h) Most institutions offering the CPE and the LPC will offer students who pass the CPE at the institution a place on their LPC.

The Legal Practice Course

(a) The Legal Practice Course will be run at a variety of institutions approved by the Law Society (at the time of publication no validation

visits have taken place to give approval to institutions to run legal practice courses).
(b) Applications for a place on a LPC are made through the Central Applications Board. Application forms are available from the CAB and should be completed and returned to the CAB not later than 31st December of the year before you wish to commence the LPC. It is the student's responsibility to ensure his/her application is returned to the CAB before the closing date. The address of the CAB is: Central Applications Board for the Legal Practice Course, Admail 44, London, SW1P 1YL.
(c) Unless taking time off after your degree you must join the Law Society before starting the LPC.
(d) Get the student enrolment form from the Law Society early in your third year and return it to the Law Society by 1st April of the year in which you intend to start the LPC.
(e) References are asked for and followed up. Make sure those whose names you give are happy to act as referees.
(f) Contact the Law Society if no reply is received by August.
(g) On graduating or passing the CPE, obtain a Certificate of Completion of the Academic Stage Training from the Law Society.
(h) Apply for a grant from your local authority.
(i) If you apply for a loan from a bank through the Law Society you will be given a more sympathetic hearing.
(j) The course is tough.
(k) It cannot be crammed because assessment takes place during the course, so attend the lectures and make use of your own notes.

Colleges providing recognized courses for the CPE

The College of Law at London (Chancery Lane, Lancaster Gate), Guildford, Chester and York (NB: all enquiries should be addressed to the Registrar, Braboeuf Manor, St Catherines, Guildford, Surrey GU3 1HA.) Tel: 0483-576711
Birmingham Polytechnic, Franchise Street, Perry Barr, Birmingham B42 2SU. Tel: 021-331 5000
Birmingham University, Law Division, PO Box 363, Birmingham B15 2TT. Tel: 021-414 6432
Bournemouth Polytechnic, Dorset House, Talbot Campus, Fernbarrow, Poole, Dorset DH12 3DB. Tel: 0202-524111

Bristol Polytechnic, Coldharbour Lane, Bristol BS16 1QY. Tel: 0272-656261
The Polytechnic of Central London, Law Department, Red Lion Square, London WC1R 4SR. Tel: 071-911 5000
The City of London Polytechnic, 84 Moorgate, London EC2M 6SQ. Tel: 071-283 1030
City University, Northampton Square, London EC1V 0HB. Tel: 071-253 4399
Coventry Polytechnic, School of Business, Priory Street, Coventry CV1 5FB. Tel: 0203-631313
Huddersfield Polytechnic, Queensgate, Huddersfield HD1 3DH. Tel: 0484-422288
Lancashire Polytechnic, Preston PR1 2TQ. Tel: 0772-201201
Leeds Polytechnic, Vernon Road, Leeds LS1 3HE. Tel: 0532-832600
Leicester Polytechnic, PO Box 143, Leicester LE1 9BH. Tel: 0533-551551
Manchester Polytechnic, Chester Street, Manchester M1 5GD. Tel: 061-228 6171
Middlesex Polytechnic, Middlesex Business School, The Burroughs, London NW4 4BT. Tel: 081-202 6545
Newcastle-upon-Tyne Polytechnic, Ellison Building, Ellison Place, Newcastle-upon-Tyne NE1 8ST. Tel: 091-232 6002
Polytechnic of North London, School of Law, 62-66 Ladbrooke House, Highbury Grove, London N5 2AD. Tel: 071-607 2789 Ext 5135
Nottingham Polytechnic, Burton Street, Nottingham NG1 4BU. Tel: 0602-418418
Staffordshire Polytechnic, College Road, Stoke on Trent ST4 2DE. Tel: 0782-744531
University of Sussex, Arts Building, Falmer, Brighton BN1 9QN. Tel: 0273-606755
The Polytechnic of Wales, Pontypridd, Mid Glamorgan CF37 1DL. Tel: 0443-480480
West London Polytechnic, St Mary's Road, Ealing, London W5 5RF. Tel: 081-579 4111
Wolverhampton Polytechnic, Arthur Storer Building, Molineux Street, Wolverhampton WV1 1SA. Tel: 0902-313002.

Articles

(a) This is a two-year practical apprenticeship usually served with a firm when you are classified a trainee solicitor.
(b) The Law Society imposes and enforces minimum standards to ensure a broad training.
(c) Inevitably your training will reflect the size, location and specialization of the practice.
(d) Large firms have a formal training structure and you are usually rotated through various departments on a series of six-month secondments.
(e) In small firms there is a more informal approach.
(f) During articles you must attend and pass a Professional Skills Course.

Finding articles

(a) There is a demand for high quality trainee solicitors.
(b) However, most students make multiple applications and so the more popular firms can afford to conduct a rigorous selection procedure.
(c) The key is information, presentation and timing.
(d) Find out which firms you want to approach using ROSET (the Register of Solicitors Employing Trainees, a Law Society publication listing over 3,000 firms and other organizations with brief relevant details), law magazines, the Law Society's Careers & Recruitment Service (see page 174), and any personal contacts. The law is a 'people' business and so this last is often the most effective.
(e) The Law Society Code of Practice says no firm should recruit trainee solicitors more than two years ahead.
(f) Most big firms therefore expect you to apply two years ahead!
(g) If reading law, this means large law firms mount a roadshow giving presentations in the spring and expect you to apply in the summer vacation of your second year.
(h) Medium sized and smaller practices, often unsure of their requirements, frequently recruit nearer the time.
(i) Identify a short list of target firms.
(j) Send each a CV (or obtain an application form from your careers service) and a brief covering letter requesting an interview.

The Code of Practice

(a) No interviewing programme for the recruitment of applicants should be initiated before 1st September in the student's final year of degree studies.

(b) Where representatives of firms of solicitors visit universities or polytechnics to interview applicants, such visits should not start before the beginning of the October term and dates of proposed visits should be agreed in advance with the appropriate careers service in each case.

(c) Ideally, an offer of articles to an undergraduate should not be subject to a time limit for acceptance. If, however, such an offer does not state a final date by which a decision is required (or by which the offer, if not accepted, will be deemed to be declined), that date should not be before 1st November in the academic year in which the law graduate takes degree finals (or the non-law graduate the CPE course) or the expiry of three weeks after the offer is sent, whichever is the latter.

(d) Students will be expected to acknowledge within a day or two the receipt of any offer and if they are able immediately to give a final acceptance or rejection then they should do so. It will, however, be open for the student when acknowledging receipt to indicate that he or she wishes to have time to consider the offer and to state the date by which it is anticipated that a final decision can be given. If such a date is outside the time limit prescribed in the offer, the firm concerned should give sympathetic consideration to extending the time limit accordingly.

(e) Students will be expected not to accumulate offers. These should be dealt with as promptly as possible and students should restrict the number of outstanding offers held at any one time to no more than two. Once a student has accepted an offer, he should tell all other employers to whom applications have been sent and thereafter he should make no further applications.

Information and statistics

Introduction

The information and statistics set out in this chapter and the one in part IV are extracts from the Annual Statistical Report of the Law Society. The report was compiled by Stephen Harwood of the Law Society's Research and Policy Planning Unit who has produced quite the most comprehensive analysis of the profession available to date. What follows here can only be a subjective selection and for a fuller and thus more accurate picture, it is recommended that a copy of the report is purchased at £14.50 from Chancery Lane.

Summary

- As at 31st July 1991 there were 68,971 solicitors on the Roll of Solicitors maintained by the Law Society. Of these seventy-four per cent were men and twenty-six per cent women.
- There were 57,167 solicitors holding a current practising certificate entitling them to act as a solicitor. Of these seventy-five per cent were men and twenty-five per cent were women.
- Of the 57,167 solicitors holding a current practising certificate, 48,152 (eighty-four per cent) were in private practice and seventy-seven per cent of these were men and twenty-three per cent were women.
- Apart from private practice, three other significant areas of employment for solicitors holding a practising certificate were commerce and industry, local government and the Crown Prosecution Service (CPS) employing 2,678, 2,394 and 1,236 solicitors respectively (representing eleven per cent of solicitors holding a practising certificate).
- At 31st July 1991 there were 13,548 separate organizations employing solicitors in England and Wales of which 10,243 were private practice solicitors' firms. Other organizations employing solicitors included local government, commerce and industry and the Crown Prosecution Service.
- Just under a half of the 10,243 solicitors' firms in private practice were based in the South East of England at 31st July 1991, with a quarter of all

firms being based in London. These figures remain virtually unchanged on last year.
- The gross fees, or turnover to the profession for the year to 31st March 1990 was £4,455 million, an increase of seventeen per cent on the previous year. Some growth in turnover will be due to an expansion in legal business and solicitor's overheads also increased by an estimated fourteen per cent over the same period. Provisional figures available for the year to 31st March 1991 show a further increase, with gross fees estimated to be about £5,169 million. This represented an increase of about sixteen per cent on 1989–90, but the rate of increase is in decline and outside of London, particularly in the South, it appears that gross fees have declined in real terms. Following adjustments for inflation and the increase in legal business we note a more modest real increase in gross fees for the profession and what evidence there is on overheads suggests that firms' profit margins may be minimal.
- Average gross fees per fee-earner rose to £64,300 in 1989–90, an increase of thirteen per cent on the previous year. With solicitor's overheads estimated to have increased by about fourteen per cent over the same period, this suggests a decline in fees in real terms. The provisional figure for 1990–91 suggests that average gross fees per fee-earner will have increased to £73,500 in 1990–91, an increase of about fourteen per cent on 1989–90.
- For the year 1st April 1990 to 31st March 1991, total legal aid payments to solicitors amounted to £562.4 million, or 11.1 per cent of the total estimated turnover of solicitors in private practice.
- In 1990–91 the proportion of transfers into the profession increased with overseas solicitors, barristers and Scottish and Northern Irish solicitors representing twenty-three per cent (962) of the 4,265 new solicitors admitted to the Roll.

Solicitors on the Roll

As at 31st July 1991 there were 68,971 solicitors on the Roll. Of these 50,972 (seventy-four per cent) were men and 17,985 (twenty-six per cent) were women. In just fourteen cases, the solicitor's sex cannot be identified on the Law Society computerized records. Last year seventy-six per cent of solicitors on the Roll were men and twenty-four per cent women.

Solicitors on the Roll with and without practising certificates by sex as at 31st July 1991

With practising certificates	Number	% with certificate	% on Roll
Men	42,986	(75.2%)	62.3%
Women	14,179	(24.8%)	20.6%
Sex unknown	2	(0.0%)	0.0%
Sub-total	57,167	(100.0%)	82.9%

Without practising certificates	Number	% without certificate	
Men	7,986	(67.7%)	11.6%
Women	3,806	(32.2%)	5.5%
Sex unknown	12	(0.1%)	0.0%
Sub-total	11,804	(100.0%)	17.1%
Total solicitors on the Roll	**68,971**		**100.0%**

Practising certificate holders

At 31st July 1991 there were 57,167 solicitors holding current practising certificates, an increase of 4.4 per cent on the previous year's number. Of these, 14,179 (twenty-five per cent) were women and 42,986 (seventy-five per cent) were men. A detailed breakdown of the types of employment of practising certificate holders is given overleaf.

Solicitors' employment

At 31st July 1991 there were 13,682 separate organizations employing solicitors of which 13,584 were based in England and Wales and ninety-eight elsewhere (ie Scotland, Northern Ireland, the Isle of Man, Eire and overseas countries). Of these 13,584 organizations employing solicitors in England and Wales, 10,243 were private practice firms.

Practising certificate holders category of employment as at 31st July 1991 (and nonpractising certificate holders category of employment where known)

Category of Employment	Total	Men	Women	(No PC*)
Private practice	48,152**	36,851	11,299	(741)
Commerce/Industry	2,678	1,987	691	(578)
Local government	2,394	1,594	800	(142)
Crown Prosecution Service (CPS)	1,263	790	473	(3)
Solicitors abroad	664	516	148	(2,023)
Locum	371	197	174	(16)
Clerk/Assistant Clerk to Justices	215	165	50	(99)
Retired	198	182	16	(3,219)
Not in active practice	148	71	77	(679)
Law Centre/Citizens Advice Bureau	113	52	61	(3)
Agent CPS	93	56	37	(1)
National undertaking	91	58	33	(10)
Government service	80	56	24	(635)
Law Society staff	69	31	38	(18)
Legal Aid Board	60	36	24	(-)
Academic	30	21	9	(420)
Other	513	304	209	(2,196)
Unknown	35	19	16	(1,021)
Total	**57,167**	**42,986**	**14,179**	**(11,804)**

* Solicitors not holding a practising certificate at 31st July 1991, but who have indicated their type of employment on annual enrolment or on their last practising certificate before ceasing to practise
** This includes two cases where the solicitor's sex was not known

Number of firms in private practice at March 1989, 1990 and 1991

Area	1989	1990	% change on 1989	Provisional 1991 figures
A: The North	3,491	3,456	−1.0%	3,371
B: The South	2,556	2,565	+0.4%	2,554
C: London	2,123	2,081	−2.0%	2,011
Non-returns*				225
Total	**8,170**	**8,102**	**−0.8%**	**8,161**

* The figures for 1991 are provisional since 225 firms (2.8%) had not submitted an annual return to LIB at the time of publication of this report

Numbers of organizations employing solicitors by type of business

Type of business	Head offices		Branch offices	
	England & Wales	Overseas	England & Wales	Overseas
Private practice	10,243	11	4,754	33
Local authority	487	0	57	0
Commerce & industry	1,507	9	384	6
National undertaking	22	0	15	0
Government service	64	2	34	0
Crown Prosecution Service	33	0	105	0
Other	1,071	76	102	5
Unknown	157	0	13	0
Total	**13,584**	**98**	**5,464**	**44**

The table following shows the changes in size of firms. It is plain that the number of large firms is increasing.

Sizes of private practice firms at March 1989, 1990 and 1991

Size of firm (by no of principals)	No of firms		% Change	Provisional 1991 figures
	1989	1990		
1	3,035	3,018	−0.6%	2,955
2–4	3,560	3,512	−1.3%	3,432
5–10	1,180	1,172	−0.7%	1,139
11+	395	400	+1.3%	410
Non returns**				225
Total	**8,170**	**8,102**	−0.8%	8,161

** The figures for 1991 are provisional since 225 firms (2.8%) had not submitted an annual return to LIB at the time of publication of this report

Private practice firms staffing as at about 31st March 1990 by size and region

It can be seen that distribution of solicitors is biased toward London, with little sign of significant change in the profession's general distribution.

Size of firm (ie number of principals)	No of firms	No of principals	Asst sols.	Other fee-earners	Admin staff	% Asst sols.	Non-sol staff per sol
London							
1	830	830	320	615	1,925	28%	2.2
2–4	848	2,202	887	1,337	5,507	29%	2.2
5–10	248	1,687	851	1,237	4,994	34%	2.5
11+	155	4,634	6,037	4,653	18,261	57%	2.1
Total	2,081	9,353	8,095	7,842	30,687	46%	2.2
South							
1	998	998	298	710	2,957	23%	2.8
2–4	1,050	2,766	855	2,064	8,632	24%	3.0
5–10	399	2,716	1,021	2,284	9,250	27%	3.1
11+	118	2,050	1,214	2,063	7,859	37%	3.0
Total	2,565	8,530	3,388	7,121	28,698	28%	3.0
North							
1	1,190	1,190	420	903	4,071	26%	3.1
2–4	1,614	4,327	1,418	2,826	13,962	25%	2.9
5–10	525	3,471	1,414	2,634	12,019	29%	3.0
11+	127	2,351	1,761	2,281	9,660	43%	2.9
Total	3,456	11,340	5,013	8,644	39,712	31%	3.0
Total	**8,102**	**29,222**	**16,496**	**23,607**	**99,097**	**36%**	**2.7**

Gross fees

Gross fees per principal includes principals who work part-time, so the gross fees per principal represent a minimum figure. Gross fees represent turnover within the profession, rather than income or profit. All overheads, including salaries, must be met out of gross fees. Without a knowledge of the level of these overheads it is not possible to establish the level of earnings of the profession.

Gross fees of firms for 1988–89, 1989–90 and 1990–91

	Gross fees £ million (% increase on previous year)		
Area	1988–89	1989–90	Provisional figures for 1990–91
A: The North	1,034 (19%)	1,209 (17%)	1,367 (13%)
B: The South	931 (21%)	1,019 (9%)	1,053 (3%)
C: London	1,831 (25%)	2,227 (22%)	2,713 (22%)
Non returns*			36
Total	**3,796 (22%)**	**4,455 (17%)**	**5,169 (16%)**

* The figures for 1991 are provisional since 225 firms (2.8%) had not submitted an annual return to LIB at the time of publication of this report. Last year these firms accounted for £36m gross fees

Gross fees per fee-earner* in private practice for the years 1987–88, 1988–89 and 1989–90

Area	1987–88 £'000	1988–89 £'000	1989–90 £'000
A: The North	39.1	43.1 (10%)	
B: The South	42.2	48.7 (15%)	
C: London	65.0	77.0 (18%)	
National average	49.2	56.8 (15%)	64.3 (13%)

* Fee earners include solicitors as well as other fee earning staff

Information and statistics

The work of the profession

Indicator	1988	1989	1990	% change on 1989
Total appeals, all courts (Judicial Statistics)	12,155	11,351	11,134	−1.9%
High Court: Proceedings commenced				
Chancery Division	27,054	30,813	42,965	+39.4%
Queen's Bench Division	235,003	288,287	373,757	+29.6%
Family Division:				
Probate	234,475	231,883	242,654	+4.6%
Wardship	3,704	4,327	4,721	+9.1%
County Court: Proceedings commenced	2,285,125	2,615,508	3,561,386	+36.2%
Crown Court, receipts:				
Committals for trial	106,524	98,668	103,011	+4.4%
Committals for sentence	8,577	8,244	8,868	+7.6%
Appeals	16,315	17,223	17,801	+3.4%
Days sat by Judges	179,549	182,957	179,554	−1.9%

Source: Lord Chancellor's Department Judicial Statistics Annual Report 1989, Cm 1154 HMSO

Part IV
The qualified career

Legal careers – a general overview
KATRINA SMITH

Katrina Smith is a Consultant with Michael Page Legal, a division of Michael Page Group PLC. She is a qualified solicitor, having trained with Dibb Lupton Broomhead in Leeds. Seeking a more commercial role, she joined the Leeds office of Michael Page Legal to coordinate recruitment in Yorkshire and following a year in the London office, she has recently taken over responsibility for legal recruitment throughout the North of England.

As both branches of the legal profession develop and diversify there is a very definite movement towards career specialization.

More recently, with the growth in solicitors' firms and the competition for good quality work, a need for lawyers with very specific experience has emerged.

This has been facilitated by the further subdivision of departments within practice generally. For example, in a large firm a company lawyer would be expected to deal only with a specific part of a transaction, a litigator would specialize in a particular field such as insurance or intellectual property work and property law can be broken down into development or leasehold work.

There is an increasing tendency to departmentalize even within the smallest firms. This may take the form of four main departments such as property, which may include conveyancing of all types, company/commercial, litigation, including personal injury and matrimonial and private client work which usually covers probate and will drafting. Even in a general practice, it is now common for an individual to indicate whether he or she wishes to handle litigious or non-litigious work.

There is no doubt that the more specialized the experience, the more in demand your skills as a lawyer will be.

Therefore, it is essential that if you wish to specialize early in your career, you gain the necessary relevant experience in articles or as soon as possible thereafter.

The most specialized and fast developing areas of law include planning and environmental law, intellectual property, pensions, construction and insolvency work. There has also been an upturn in the demand for lawyers in specialist fields such as matrimonial and tax planning.

Industry

The last five years have seen a great deal of growth in commerce and industry, both in general and from a legal perspective. This has resulted in the demand for lawyers to work in-house as legal advisers.

Opportunities in industry and commerce are open to both barristers and solicitors and cover many commercial aspects of law. The content of legal work will vary dependent upon a number of factors.

'*I want a good libel lawyer.*'

Firstly a large public company may have a substantial legal department covering all aspects of work such as company, property and litigation. Some organizations have a policy of handling certain types of work in-house and using external solicitors for more complicated specialist matters. Finally, different corporate sectors will affect the type of legal work. For example, an insurance company will tend to concentrate on litigation matters and a construction firm, upon property.

Commercial experience is usually a prerequisite for a career in industry. Prospects and salary potential are very similar to those in practice. A solicitor or barrister in industry can progress from a junior in the department through management to a group solicitor position. Alternatively, he or she may change direction to become a company secretary with a view to eventually securing a position on the board.

Appointments in industry can cover many different sectors. The most popular and fast growing sectors in the current market include banking, oil and telecommunications.

Careers outside practice or industry

As a qualified lawyer there are a large number of options available and some examples are as follows:

Local government
This offers wide experience in many aspects of local government law including planning, child care, highways and housing. Salaries are initially very good but often have a finite level and the transition from local government to private practice can be difficult. However, good planning or child care experience is very much in demand in private practice.

The magistrates' court
This provides good exposure to all aspects of magistrates' court procedure and at senior levels will create opportunities to become a magistrate's clerk.

The Crown Prosecution Service
The service is made up of both barristers and solicitors who act on a day to day basis in representing the Crown in the criminal courts. Opportunities are available from trainee positions to very experienced solicitors. The service

provides excellent advocacy and criminal litigation experience.

The forces
The army, the navy and the RAF recruit solicitors and barristers with good advocacy experience to work at home or abroad, largely handling court martial and criminal defence work.

Law centres
These deal directly with the community providing legal advice for those without access to a solicitor. Handling mainly legal aid work, the function of the law centre is similar to the citizens advice bureau.

As a lawyer, there are many diverse career opportunities to pursue both within practice, in industry and commerce and in many other sectors. A legal qualification is very valuable and even the lawyer who wishes to pursue a career outside the law can use his or her qualification as a stepping stone to other areas such as business development, lecturing or legal recruitment.

Company and commercial law
JONATHAN ELSTEIN

Nabarro Nathanson is based in London and has its own office or associations with leading law firms in the United States, Western and Eastern Europe, the Middle East, Caribbean and Australia. The firm provides a wide range of legal services including corporate and commercial matters and commercial property. Jonathan Elstein is an Assistant Solicitor in the company and commercial department.

It is part of any professional adviser's job to make themselves appear indispensable to their client. However, it would be hard to dispute that almost all substantial commercial transactions benefit from the attention of a suitably expert lawyer. Fortunately for the health of the profession, most companies and businessmen realize this and have come to rely on their corporate lawyers when formulating and implementing any significant commercial objective.

The fields of expertise open to a company and commercial lawyer are as varied as the areas of commerce itself. It is a function of governments in developed countries to regulate conduct between citizens; and since commerce affects virtually all of us in some capacity, it is unsurprising to find it highly regulated. The purpose of regulation is arguably not so much to provide a perfectly just solution to all possible problems as to create an environment of commercial certainty where rights and obligations can be predicted and in which the business world can thus properly operate (the idea being that in an efficient market, certainty itself leads to justice).

The sources of company law are various. Historically, many of the rules governing the conduct of company directors developed from nineteenth-century ideas about the obligations of trustees, since directors were perceived as owing similar fiduciary obligations towards their company. Today, however, the growth of commerce (particularly the development of sophisticated markets for shares and other securities and the globalization of trade) has led to a proliferation of rules and regulations. Some of these are enacted directly by Parliament, but other bodies such as The Panel on Takeovers and Mergers can be equally important. It is the task of corporate lawyers to guide their client through the various hoops without ever losing sight of the commercial objectives the client is seeking to achieve.

It is misleading, however, to talk of 'the client' as if all clients behaved similarly. Nabarro Nathanson is typical of the larger UK commercial practices in that it acts for a great range of clients. On one extreme there are international governments, leading property and industrial companies, banks, professional advisers and other large public and private companies. At the other extreme we act for those starting small new ventures or buying existing small businesses from their present owners.

There are, however, certain characteristics common to most work carried out by a company/commercial department. First, complete technical competence is expected by the client. This means that a significant part of the lawyer's time must be devoted to keeping up with the latest developments not only in pure company law but also in the fields of tax, pensions, EC law and so on. Secondly, however, to be most effective the lawyer must be able to see beyond the technical position to the commercial goal. Clients rarely appreciate being told that their objectives are unattainable, whereas they are always interested to learn if those objectives can be achieved more effectively by some innovative scheme. Thirdly, it is a function of high value corporate transactions that those involved with them tend to work under a great deal of pressure. The amounts involved in such transactions coupled with the short timescale usually available may result in frenetic work for most hours of the day and night, possibly for a number of weeks. These pressures have also led firms to invest in state-of-the-art technology.

It is a cliché to add that such pressures increase the sense of satisfaction when a transaction is complete, but like most clichés this contains a large measure of truth. The fact that many transactions require the corporate lawyer to work in a team not only with lawyers from other fields but also with accountants, merchant bankers and PR advisers, tends to add to a feeling of achievement (as does the fact that larger transactions are often reported in the national press).

To summarize, there is no single quality which makes one a successful corporate lawyer; and it is equally difficult for those practising in this field to pinpoint its attraction for them. However, to paraphrase Aristotle's comment on elephants, the inability to define something does not always prevent you from recognizing it when you see it.

Practising in planning law
ELAINE A DRIVER

Elaine A Driver is a Senior Assistant in the planning group of the property department at Frere Cholmeley, a leading European law firm offering a full range of commercial legal services from its offices in London, Paris, Rome, Milan, Barcelona, Brussels, Monte Carlo and Berlin. Elaine joined Frere Cholmeley upon qualification in 1987 having been articled in local government.

Planning law is an area of specialization which is increasingly recognized in its own right and is no longer just part of the property department or a limb of the litigation department. Most major law firms now have their own planning departments. In local government it has always been an important function in the legal department of any council.

It is an area relatively unknown to many students embarking on a legal career. Colleges which feature planning law as a course subject are the exception rather than the norm. The Law Society still only allocates a few pages of its Finals course material to planning law; this is an inadequate reflection of the importance of the subject, which by its very nature infringes upon everyday life to varying degrees.

Aspects of planning law can range from the installation of a domestic satellite dish to the construction of an 'out of town' retail centre. The difference in value of land with or without the benefit of planning permission will often be huge and therefore great importance is attached to obtaining the grant of planning permission.

A planning lawyer would lead a relatively simple life if he or she merely needed to consider the planning legislation to advise clients upon the likely success of obtaining a planning consent. However, any planning decision is made against the backdrop of central government policy and guidance, local policies in development plans and planning decisions made by inspectors on appeal. These must all be understood and digested by the planning lawyer. Add to this the local politics involved in making any planning decision and the result is a varied and often high profile task of balancing competing interests.

Public pressure groups are increasingly willing and able to challenge the decisions of the Secretary of State's or local council on planning questions by way of judicial review. The battle by Save Britain's Heritage over the proposal by Peter Palumbo to demolish No 1 Poultry in the City of London is a good example. The possibility of success of similar challenges by interested bodies is yet another aspect for a planning lawyer to consider.

Developments will often involve considerations of highway law, compulsory purchase and compensation issues which are all necessary parts of a planning lawyer's working brief. The increasing importance of environmental and conservation issues and EC legislation is an added dimension; evidence the recent intervention of the EC in the proposed M3 link. To be an effective planning lawyer one must have a working understanding of the interaction of planning law with the environmental legislation and in particular the need for environmental assessments on proposed large scale developments.

The scope of work covered by a planning lawyer can range from the seeking of planning permission, participation in the preparation of development plans, advising on the legality of an enforcement notice which is served against a purported breach of planning control, the negotiation of planning agreements to considerations as to whether planning permission is required in the first place.

What skills then does a planning lawyer need?

- A good understanding of the law and policies together with a capacity to keep up-to-date with the constantly changing policies and often law on the subject.
- A working appreciation of how administration at local and central government level works and how it interacts with local and national politics.
- The skills of an advocate in putting the case either for or against a proposed development, primarily before an inspector at a public local inquiry on appeal.
- The patience and tact of a diplomat in dealing with councillors, planning officers, local residents and pressure groups.
- An ability to coordinate teams of professionals from planning consultants and surveyors to landscape architects and highway engineers who may all be involved in a proposed development. The satisfaction of successful teamwork should not be underestimated.

- Skills of crafting and interpreting planning documents.

The public's increasing awareness of local and national environmental issues will lead to greater participation and interest in planning decisions at both local and national levels. Such heightened awareness and the growing importance of environmental controls will inevitably result in the work of planning lawyers becoming more demanding and interesting.

Criminal law
DAVID SAVAGE

David Savage, who was admitted in 1963, is a Partner in the firm of Foster Savage & Gordon of Farnborough, and a member of the Council of The Law Society.

There is a feeling of unease around that there is something wrong with the criminal justice system. Public confidence is at a low ebb, following a number of successful appeals, which have attracted a great deal of media coverage. The Government's response has been to establish a Royal Commission, but it will be some while before it reports and still longer before legislative changes are made. Some lawyers have said nothing short of root and branch surgery will suffice. In short, its critics say, the adversarial system must go. In its place, they advocate adopting what they call of the best of the inquisitorial system, by giving the court and therefore the judge a more involved role in the investigation process. Its proponents say such a system would elicit the truth. Not necessarily so is the retort, and anyway, what is the aim of the criminal justice system? To prove the case against the defendant beyond all reasonable doubt or to establish the truth? The two may not necessarily be the same.

Whatever system exists the role of the solicitor is crucial. He will gather the evidence and decide the thrust of the presentation of the case. For those solicitors primarily involved in defence work, then involvement would be at the outset, from the moment of the arrest of the suspect. It is little known that everyone – irrespective of means – is entitled to free legal assistance if called to a police station for questioning. Many solicitors who accept cases for defendants will be on a 24 hour-duty call-out rota. When the telephone rings in the early hours of the morning – there is no telling the nature of the problem; it may be a matter which warrants advice over the telephone, or it could be to advise on the most serious crime in the criminal calendar. Much of the work of defence solicitors is publicly funded. The financial rewards do not compare with those available, in good times, for commercial lawyers but the job satisfaction is immense.

No field of legal practice can offer such variety and challenges. Frequently, quick thinking is required, and always a positive approach. This applies equally to the defending solicitor, and to the prosecutor. Since its establishment as a government department in 1986, the stature of the Crown Prosecution Service has grown: its standards are high and exacting. The career opportunities are continually being improved.

Over the years the pattern of private practice has changed. Some say we face an uncertain future. There must be changes, as solicitors come to exercise wider rights of audience, which they expect to be granted. The Legal Aid Board will make a wider impact on the manner in which we work. As efforts are made to curb rising costs, the desire by the Legal Aid Board for franchising (giving of monopoly to one or a few firms in an area) of Legal Aid work will grow. More likely, the solicitors who wish to undertake a heavier advocacy case load, is for them to practise as sole practitioners, sharing with others overhead expenses but without being in partnership. Times are changing – the challenges are there and for those embarking on such a career, the rewards, the greatest of which will be job satisfaction.

Working overseas
SIMON MARTIN

Simon Martin is a Solicitor in the company, commercial and banking department of Macfarlanes. He joined the firm in 1984 and spent three months, during articles, with a US law firm. Since July 1990, he has been on secondment to the Tokyo office of O'Melveny & Myers, a US law firm with whom Macfarlanes has a strategic alliance.

As industry and commerce have become increasingly international in character, with the emergence of global markets for goods and services, so solicitors in the UK have had to consider how best to provide comprehensive international legal services for their clients. The result has been an ever-expanding network of strategic alliances between lawyers in different jurisdictions and the opening of overseas offices in locations as diverse as Brussels, New York, Tokyo and Moscow.

In consequence, English solicitors now have more opportunities than ever before to work abroad, either on secondment to foreign law firms or at their own firm's overseas offices.

Secondments

Many UK law firms have now established links, formal or informal, with foreign law firms in the belief that to obtain the best advice for a client in a foreign jurisdiction, it is necessary to use local lawyers. These links have also given individual solicitors the chance to work with a foreign correspondent firm. The purpose of the secondment may be to maintain and strengthen the relationship between the two firms, to gain experience of working with foreign clients and different legal systems or to win new business. Usually it will be a combination of these factors.

The solicitor will usually work under the supervision of a partner of the host law firm, assisting on local transactions and occasionally advising on matters of English law. The period of secondment can be for anything from three months to a year or more, depending on the circumstances.

Overseas offices

A solicitor working in his or her firm's own overseas offices will generally spend a greater part of his or her time advising local clients on English law. A second and equally important role is to assist UK clients investing or trading in the foreign country by working closely with local lawyers or, where permitted, employing locally qualified lawyers. The ability to attract and service local clients is vital to the success of the office. A qualified solicitor working at an overseas office can expect the assignment to run for three to five years. A shorter period would not allow the solicitor sufficient time to understand local business practices or establish worthwhile relationships with existing and potential clients.

Feast or famine

The number of lawyers in an overseas office can vary considerably, depending on the number of local clients, the needs of UK-based clients operating in that jurisdiction and the range of legal services which are offered. Many firms in the City of London now offer trainee solicitors the opportunity to spend up to six months working in an overseas office where they will join a sizeable team of qualified solicitors. At the other end of the scale, a number of English firms with offices in Tokyo are represented by a single partner, bravely flying the flag.

The volume of work may fluctuate markedly – in a small office, a single large deal can impose great strains and pressures on both lawyers and support staff. On the other hand, it may take some years to establish a solid local client base, generating a constant flow of work so that the lawyer may find himself with a great deal of time to devote to research and business development lunches!

Where possible, negotiations, drafting and research are undertaken in the overseas office, but on larger, more complex matters close liaison with and assistance from head office is often essential. In these circumstances, the staff in the overseas office will work long hours to bridge the time difference with London using telephones, fax machines and automatic document transfers.

The attractions

Whether on secondment or working in the foreign office of an English law firm, working overseas offers a professional and personal challenge. The

'Can I do the conveyancing?'

solicitor will be expected to take on significant responsibilities both in his or her legal practice and also, perhaps, in the running of the office. The experience of living and working in a foreign country, with the opportunity to develop language skills and learn about an alien culture can be very rewarding.

1992 and beyond

It is inevitable that the international practice of law will continue to develop rapidly and more opportunities will arise for English solicitors to work overseas. The collapse of communism and the development of a free market economy in Eastern Europe and the Soviet Union have caused a number of law firms to open offices, either alone or in conjunction with local lawyers.

In the European Community, the EC Directive on professional qualifications, when fully implemented, will enable qualified professionals from one member state to practise in any other member state without requalifying.

In the UK, the internationalization of law has been recognized in the publication, during the spring of 1991, of the Law Society's draft rules on multinational partnerships which aim to permit solicitors in England and Wales to form partnerships with foreign lawyers. These measures will provide new challenges for the English legal profession and new opportunities for English lawyers to work abroad.

A career in taxation
JOHN AVERY JONES CBE

John Avery Jones is Senior Partner of Speechly Bircham, a thirty partner firm of solicitors, and has specialized in taxation for over twenty-five years. He is also joint editor of the *British Tax Review* and chairman of the International Bureau of Fiscal Documentation in Amsterdam.

There should be nothing surprising in finding taxation listed in this book as a subject for a legal career. Taxation is not, as is sometimes thought, a branch of accounting; it is a normal legal subject which rests primarily on familiar legal skills of dealing with statutory interpretation and case law. It is not even particularly concerned with figures; no mathematical expertise is required for a legal career in tax, although an ability to read accounts, which may be self-taught, is an advantage. It is also most unlikely that the work will involve filling in tax returns.

The main interest of tax as a career is, contrary to expectations, the variety of legal problems which arise. The reason is that a tax problem never exists in the abstract but always relates to another legal discipline. The problem itself may concern company law, property law (particularly with VAT on commercial property transactions), trusts, European law (particularly so with VAT, but this is beginning to apply to direct taxes as well), or almost any other legal subject. A good tax lawyer needs to be familiar with all these branches of the law, and very familiar with any legal area of which he specializes in the tax aspects. One must, for example, know the limitations of company law in suggesting courses of action in connection with a company reconstruction. One cannot answer a tax point about an EEIG without a full understanding of what an EEIG is. And one cannot interpret a VAT directive without a knowledge of the methods of interpretation used generally by the European Court. Often the tax effects of a transaction are simple once the problem has been properly analysed in terms of the underlying law. Tax work is increasingly international, involving fitting together two or more different tax systems which were never designed to be fitted together.

A solicitor dealing with tax will normally divide his time between answering questions from his colleagues who are dealing with transactions in which there is a tax angle, part of which involves training colleagues to recognize when there might be a tax problem and asking the question before it is too late, and dealing directly with clients in exactly the same way as other solicitors. Dealing with internal questions often requires the ability to give instant or almost instant answers. There is often considerable liaison with the Revenue Bar both for advisory work and litigation. Tax departments tend to be much smaller than say, commercial departments of firms of solicitors, which gives more scope for able individuals to do important and interesting work with a high intellectual content at an early stage in their career.

Tax appeals give opportunities, unfortunately not as often taken as they should be, for advocacy before the special or general commissioners of income tax and the VAT tribunal, which solicitors are more suited to doing than accountants from their training. Appeals to the higher courts on points of law give the normal scope for solicitors to prepare cases and brief counsel. Tax cases are more likely than most types of cases to be fought rather than settled, and often reach the Court of Appeal or the House of Lords.

One of the difficulties of tax for those starting in it is the volume of the statutory materials: not only a Taxes Act 1988 with 845 sections and 31 schedules, but also separate acts dealing with capital gains, capital allowances, stamp duty, inheritance tax, oil taxation and VAT, and annual finance acts in addition, to say nothing of sixty volumes of tax cases and a growing quantity of statements of practice and other non-statutory material. This should not put anyone off and it is surprising how quickly people manage to become familiar with those parts of it which they need to know. A good memory is an essential requirement, and this is normally backed up with electronic retrieval.

The work of an intellectual property solicitor

MARK LUBBOCK

Mark Lubbock read Natural Sciences (Part I) and Law (Part II) at Cambridge University and qualified as a solicitor in 1984 after completing his articles with a leading London firm. He joined Ashurst Morris Crisp, a leading City firm, in 1988 where he is now a Senior Associate practising intellectual property law.

Intellectual property rights are increasingly recognized as a vital part of the assets of any business. The protection, maintenance, exploitation and, where appropriate, acquisition or transfer of these assets can be central to the business' value and profitability. It is part of the job of the intellectual property solicitor to ensure that this is carried out effectively.

What is intellectual property?

Intellectual property describes a mixed bundle of various rights which protect different aspects of human creative skill and effort. In the United Kingdom, the most important types of statute-based intellectual property rights are patents, copyrights, unregistered design rights, registered designs and registered trade or service marks. There are also rights which derive from the common law such as rights to prevent a person from 'passing off' his goods as those of another and rights to prevent the unauthorized use or disclosure of confidential information. In many cases these rights will provide a business with a monopoly or quasi-monopoly in relation to various features of its products or services, enabling the owner of the rights to prevent others from copying them. The exercise of such 'monopolistic' rights often conflicts with pro-competitive laws – particularly those relating to the free movement of goods throughout the European Community. It is this conflict which is giving rise to some of the most interesting legal and economic issues in intellectual property law. The European Commission has focused on the issue of intellectual property as being central to the single European market and has initiated proposals to harmonize national laws. This is resulting in extensive changes to UK intellectual property law.

The work

The work of an intellectual property solicitor covers an extraordinary width of subject-matter because of the variety of the rights involved. Patents protect inventions of any sort which are capable of industrial application, from dieting schemes to genetically engineered organisms. Copyright protects original works such as books, plays, music, works of art, sound recordings and films. Unregistered design rights protect the original designs of articles (usually of an industrial nature) which do not themselves attract copyright protection like electric plugs or door handles. Registered designs can be used to protect the appearance of articles designed to have 'eye appeal' like shoes or table lamps.

Trade and service marks and rights of passing off protect the reputation of a business or a product which is often closely associated with its trade name or the style of its packaging. An example of a famous registered trademark is 'Coca-Cola', and although the courts refused a registration for the shape of a 'Coca-Cola' bottle, it would be protected by rights of passing off. Rights of confidence are used to protect a company's trade secrets which could consist of anything from a secret drug formula to customer lists.

Because of the specialized nature of intellectual property law, intellectual property solicitors are usually expected to be capable of carrying out both contentious (ie litigious) and noncontentious work, although in practical terms, many solicitors will tend to concentrate in one area or the other depending upon their preferences and the availability of work as they become more senior.

On the contentious side, the work covers the complete spectrum of litigation from urgent applications to the courts, to massive actions drawn out over many years. Because of the value and fragility of intellectual property rights, it is often important for the owner of the rights to obtain orders at short notice from the courts to seize evidence or to restrain the infringement. At the other end of the spectrum, the work can consist of running massive actions (usually patents-based) which can take several years to resolve, often involving huge sums of money, several jurisdictions and rooms full of documents. A recent example of such an action is the litigation between Kodak and Polaroid relating to the patents protecting 'instant' picture technology.

On the noncontentious side, the work varies from fielding requests from clients for advice on intellectual property (how can I protect my idea? will I be sued for marketing this product?), to the drafting and negotiation of licences and commercial agreements, such as those relating to computer software. In addition, the intellectual property lawyer may be called upon to undertake audits of a business' intellectual property rights prior to its disposal or acquisition and to draft and negotiate the agreement governing the sale or purchase of these rights.

The intellectual property solicitor is also often seen by others in his or her firm as capable of handling any unusual matter on which the firm is required to advise. Accordingly, the work often involves advising on and drafting agreements in relation to areas of the law in respect of which intellectual property only has a passing reference such as broadcasting or telecommunications.

The lawyers

The most important attribute of an intellectual property lawyer is his or her adaptability. The law relating to each type of intellectual property right have a number of common features but are essentially different, and, because of the wide range of subject-matter, the lawyer must be equally able to advise on one day in relation to, for example, patent law for a heavy engineering application and the next on exploitation of the copyright in a television programme.

Linked to this ability to adapt is the need to be on top of your subject. Intellectual property law has traditionally been undertaught at university and it is important to apply yourself in the early stages of your career, in order to acquire the detailed knowledge of the existing law that is necessary if you are properly to protect your clients' interests.

Since intellectual property rights are so important to your client's business, it is necessary to be able to understand not only the law and the subject-matter of the rights, but also how your client's business operates and what it is that he wants to achieve commercially. Often the lawyer will have much greater experience of commercial negotiations than his client and will be expected not only to know the law and draft the agreement, but also to close the deal!

Private client work in a large firm
JUSTIN APPLEYARD

Justin Appleyard is an Assistant Solicitor in the City Private Client Department of Penningtons. He has been qualified for a year.

Private client work in a large firm is often thought to be the dreaming up of clever devices to avoid inheritance tax. Certainly, reducing the impact of taxation is a very important aspect of what you do. But deciding on the most tax efficient structure of achieving a client's wishes comes during and sometimes after helping the client to decide what his plans are.

It is as important to get to know the client well and to find out not only what he earns and owns (and might earn or own in the future) but also how secure he feels about his old age and his spouse's security if he dies before her. You have to discover (gently) if he has any private concerns about, for example, his children, and whether they will have enough money when they really need it or too much when they are not old enough to look after it properly. Or he may be more worried about his own parents if they survive him. The only certainty is that there is no single answer for any client.

Our city private client department specializes in creative estate planning, and it is in search of this that many wealthy clients still look to the larger London firm. This kind of work means putting together a scheme that makes full provision for your client even if he loses his job or becomes very ill, while it also provides for the rest of his family (and anyone else whom he wants to benefit) in such a way that tax is kept to a minimum. But you have to remember that both the personal and fiscal reasons for the scheme could change without any warning. Flexibility is essential as are frequent reviews to make sure that the balance between your client's aims and the tax consequences of achieving them stays in your client's favour.

Your client will often be a client of other departments of your firm. Sometimes the company department may act for his company and introduce him to you – perhaps when his company is being substantially restructured so that he is about to become much wealthier. In these circumstances, a new will is probably appropriate and possibly some more elaborate arrangements if the client can afford to give away some of his newly acquired wealth. This process also works in reverse. The private client department will have clients who at first ask for your help in your field only. But the plan that is finally chosen may involve, for example, creating different classes of shares in his company. Then it would be your turn to introduce your client to the company department. The same applies to property matters and occasionally to clients of the litigation department. Nearly every one of your clients will own a house (and possibly several, some of which may be overseas). Others will be farmers – either as tenants or as landlords. As regards litigation, it is quite possible that what you have in mind for an existing but now obsolete trust will require the consent of the court. From time to time you may have clients who need advice on criminal prosecutions brought against them or perhaps their children.

One of the advantages of being a private client lawyer in a large firm is that, unlike some young solicitors in large firms, you are still able to be involved in fields of law outside your own – indeed, this is often important. You will usually be the first person your client telephones when he needs any legal advice and you have to be able to give him at least some reassurance before you pass the matter to your colleagues. Even then, you will probably participate fully in the matter as it progresses and will still be your client's first point of contact.

If your firm also has a matrimonial and family department, then you are likely to work especially closely with those lawyers. One of the first needs of a client who is getting divorced is a new will. Frequently, however, one or both parties will have created trusts in the past or be beneficiaries of them. It might be your task to show that the financial provision offered by a husband could be more (or less) because he is, say, the life tenant of a strict settlement. Or you might be drafting a trust of a life insurance policy to reflect the terms of the agreed divorce settlement. Or you could be advising on the tax implications of the various trusts being considered as compromises of a claim by a wife not reasonably provided for under her deceased husband's will.

Our private client department is certainly small by comparison with the other departments. Because the overheads are lower, much of our probate work and our agricultural work is done in our regional offices. Even so, although the emphasis in London is on tax planning, the work is diverse and challenging. After all, you are providing a service to individuals by helping them to achieve their private as well as financial objectives. This may be by constructing complex tax avoidance schemes but more often it is by providing reassurance and practical advice so that those individuals know that their family is being, and will be, provided for.

A legal career in commerce, finance and industry
KAMLESH BAHL

Kamlesh Bahl is the Company Secretary and Manager, Legal Services for Data Logic Limited, an international software services company in the computer industry. She is a member of the Law Society's Council and non-executive member of Parkside Health Authority. She is also a member of the Law Society's Race Relations Committee and was Chairman of the Law Society's Commerce and Industry Group 1988/89, which represents all solicitors employed in commerce, finance and industry.

The concept of solicitors working in commerce, finance and industry is relatively recent in the UK. Twenty-five years ago a solicitor going into industry was regarded as 'a loss to the profession'. Equally, solicitors in industry were seen as a necessary evil and the businessman would only go to his or her in-house solicitor when it was absolutely necessary, eg when the company was sued.

Today, the image of a solicitor in industry has dramatically changed. In almost every major commercial concern there are now in-house solicitors and the demand is rapidly increasing. In fact, comparisons are now drawn between UK in-house solicitors and the 'Corporate Counsel' in the USA who have a long and well-established tradition. So what are the advantages of being an in-house solicitor?

Firstly, the in-house solicitor is required to build up a thorough and detailed understanding of the business, the personalities in it and the way industry works in general. He or she must become familiar with the policies and strategies of the company and its particular sensitivities. He or she is then uniquely placed to give legal advice which is *relevant* to that organization and to make positive recommendations which the business can implement.

Secondly, the solicitor is available, not only when an emergency arises but at other times, too. The solicitor can play a preventative role, which means that the company seeks and gets legal advice earlier and puts this into effect when formulating its long and short-term strategies and policies.

Thirdly, the in-house solicitor plays a major role in multidisciplinary teams with people of different backgrounds and skills within the company where all are trying to achieve a common objective, eg a company acquisition, a joint venture agreement.

Fourthly and increasingly, the in-house solicitor is playing a critical role as a member of the company's management team. Most companies now recognize that the logical objective and factual approach that a legal training provides are critical skills required for management.

Fifthly, the complexity of legislation, and the increasing and detailed impact it now has on every aspect of an organization's operation, means readily available legal advice is now essential.

A recent survey showed that external solicitors are approximately three-and-a-half times more expensive to employ than in-house solicitors. An in-house legal department also provides better control over legal costs where external lawyers need to be used.

Also, more and more organizations, particularly with the advent of 1992, are becoming international in their outlook. The in-house solicitor has to be able to adapt to these changes and understand different cultures and negotiating styles and, depending on the employer's business, will often get involved in overseas negotiations.

So, what benefits are there for the in-house solicitor?

- He or she gets to know and understand the business fully and becomes commercially aware. This leads to the satisfaction of giving legal advice that is clear, practical and easy to understand and tailored to that organization's business needs.
- He or she gets involved from the beginning to the end in projects, for example in every aspect of the setting up of a subsidiary company in another country. He or she would consider, with a local lawyer, the relevant laws, the establishment of the company, and the legislation concerning the business operating in that country such as employment law, pensions, leasing of premises.
- He or she will get to meet and work closely with members of other professions and disciplines, and will have to work positively and constructively to find a solution for the company which addresses concerns from all members of the team.
- The nature of the job means that there is always variety and the solicitor now has to have a wide knowledge of major developments, certainly in

UK and EC law.
- The in-house solicitor has the satisfaction of knowing that a contribution in the early stages of the company's policy formulations means that the company is acting legally and as a good corporate citizen.

The solicitor in commerce and industry is expected to be a person with good legal knowledge, who has a flexible and confident attitude and who can communicate clearly and simply. They are expected to be able to adapt, understand and help achieve a company's objectives both short and long-term. The solicitor has to be an individual who can work under pressure, to cope with unexpected and varied demands and to communicate with all levels of management within an organization. Usually the in-house solicitor operates as a general practitioner, ie to spot issues and advise generally on all areas of a company's business. However, many in-house solicitors also develop specialisms, such as employment law, intellectual property law and competition law which are relevant to the employer's business.

In-house solicitors and solicitors in private practice both have the same legal status and standing. The major difference is that, generally, in-house solicitors are employed to give advice on a full-time basis to one client, their employer. A solicitor in private practice will be retained, however, to deal with specific legal questions for a variety of clients. In practice, the in-house solicitor also has a number of clients, for example the various departments in a company such as financial, personnel, marketing and the directors of the company. In larger companies, the in-house solicitor often acts for the company's subsidiaries including overseas subsidiaries.

The avenues for career progression as a lawyer in commerce, finance and industry are also developing rapidly. There is, of course, the traditional aspiration of becoming the head of the legal department, which can now range from small to very large indeed. Another well-established career path is to become the company secretary and this usually means a place on the board. In recent years the particular contribution of in-house solicitors has been reorganized and there is now plenty of scope to develop in other management areas, eg finance, administration, marketing. There are now examples of solicitors who have achieved very high positions of responsibility in commerce, finance and industry, eg the company secretary at British Gas, and the current chairman of ICI. There are ample opportunities to develop in many different directions and into a variety of business areas to suit any particular talent or interest.

The major changes in industry in the UK, the need for greater efficiency and profitability and the need to be international in outlook, have led to major changes in the demands made of the in-house solicitor. These changes, together with the developments in the role and perception of the in-house solicitor, mean that this is a highly demanding, challenging, exciting and now critical role.

Further information about a career as a solicitor in commerce and industry can be obtained from: Juliet Heasman, Committee Secretary, The Law Society's Commerce and Industry Group, The Law Society, 113 Chancery Lane, London WC2A 1PL. Tel: 071-242 1222.

Working in a legal aid practice
ROBERTA TISH

Roberta Tish is a Legal Aid Practitioner specializing in matrimonial and family law. She is the former Chair of the Legal Aid Practitioners Group and Secretary of the Legal Aid Committee of the International Bar Association. The Legal Aid Practitioners Group provides information on, and bids for, better services in legal aid work.

Legal aid is considered by some to be the Cinderella of legal practice, but for anybody interested in law as it affects our fellow citizens, then it is a vital and fascinating area to consider working in.

There are, in fact, several complementary areas to the legal aid system. Criminal legal aid is dealt with quite separately as is matrimonial and civil non-matrimonial. There are also systems to cover work at the police stations under the Police and Criminal Evidence Act and green form advice, which extends to tribunal work which full legal aid does not cover.

Most practices have a mix of legal aid work with specialist departments, although in small towns and rural practices very often the work which is done under legal aid is done by a generalist.

Many legal aid practices have grown extremely large and are well known in their particular fields for a very specialized service. Anybody who is committed to legal aid will have to deal with a wide range of clients, many of whom have never been in contact with the law before and many others who are in deep emotional distress. The legal aid practitioner has to be tough and disciplined.

Legal aid firms who want to succeed in the 1990s are having to ensure that they can recruit trainees in competition with the large commercial firms, especially in the City of London. However, trainees going into a legal aid firm do not receive the high financial rewards that they would in such commercial firms. It is fairly well known that legal aid rates are not particularly good, but legal aid practices, as a result, are obliged to be more efficient and cost conscious than the larger City firms and as a result have a vested interest in obtaining well-qualified trainee solicitors and investing in information technology and management programmes that will ensure that the money they make is put to the best use.

At the moment, in Birmingham there is an experiment being carried out by the Legal Aid Board into what is known as 'franchising'. This has enormous implications for the future of the profession because solicitors who get a Legal Aid Board 'franchise' will in fact have the imprimatur to say that they are quality practitioners with specialist knowledge in the areas in which their 'franchise' is granted.

Because of the necessity for quality in legal aid firms, legal aid practitioners in particular need trainees who not only have the interest of legally aided clients at heart but who are exceptionally competent. The trainee in a legal aid practice will be expected to undergo further training both on-the-job and in special training sessions, either inside or outside the practice. However, it is not to be thought that because the firm has a 'franchise' in a particular speciality that other areas of law and legal aid practice will be ignored and a trainee can expect a wide spectrum of subjects with which to become acquainted.

Legal aid practice covers crime, family work, Children Act work, tribunal work, personal injury and medical negligence work as well as housing and welfare law. Obviously, not every practice will cover all of these areas; some specializing in one or two only as well as perhaps a mix of domestic conveyancing, probate and commercial work. A lot of legal aid work comes to solicitors through the advice agencies and many solicitors expect their trainees to become involved with such agencies by doing voluntary work on a rota system and maintaining thereby an interest in the local community. Clearly, with this kind of work and local commitment, legal aid firms are not like the large commercial practices, either in the type of client they represent or very often in the internal structures of the firm. In many legal aid practices, trainees are expected quite early on in their training to take on a caseload and be responsible for dealing with clients by taking instructions, and are encouraged to appear before those courts which give them right of audience, which is a valuable asset for those trainees who wish to become advocates.

The legal profession and particularly the legal aid sector is a rapidly changing one and would provide a rewarding career structure for those trainees who see their future in a people-oriented practice.

If you have decided that work in such a practice would be of interest to you, then information can be obtained from the law departments of polytechnics and universities, and very often the local Law Society can also provide information about legal aid practices which are looking for articled clerks. In addition, the Legal Aid Practitioners Group has a list of their members, all of whom are running legal aid practices and who are often looking for suitable trainees. The Law Society in London also maintains a register of practitioners who are looking for trainees and where it is a legal aid practice, they mention this fact.

If you have a genuine interest in helping people and seek a really satisfying career, albeit with lower financial rewards than you might find in the City, then you may well find that a legal aid practice is exactly what you are looking for.

The Government Legal Service

The Government Legal Service consists of about 950 lawyers – both solicitors and barristers – who between them provide a full range of services for the government of the day. They work in all the major departments of state, as well as some smaller, more specialized departments.

It is impossible here to touch on more than a few activities of the GLS, whose work embraces virtually every aspect of the law you would expect to meet in a private law firm, as well as some unique work of national or international importance. There are few areas of the law in which the government does not have a crucial interest, and its lawyers are closely involved in the legislative process. They instruct Parliamentary Counsel on the preparation of primary legislation, themselves draft secondary legislation, and follow Bills through Parliament, advising ministers and policy administrators at each stage as necessary. Thus they may find themselves closely involved in matters which are sometimes controversial, and often make the headlines. Even the litigation work can have a very high profile, and there is plenty of scope for high quality advocacy. Other posts in the GLS offer a different perspective of more familiar areas of the law, such as property or employment law. The government is one of the largest landowners and employers in the country, and all the consequent legal work is done in-house. Much GLS work brings with it a satisfying sense of public service, for example in the fields of consumer protection or health and safety.

Most of our lawyers join after qualification, and all posts in the GLS are open to both branches of the profession. We also offer articles or pupillage to a small number of top quality legal trainees. Sponsorship is available.

The GLS has a clearly-defined grading structure. Promotability is assessed impartially as part of a continuous appraisal of individual performance. Salary is regularly reviewed and offers opportunities for performance-related increments beyond the maxima of salary scales. An attractive non-contributory pension scheme, generous paid leave allowance and the domestic advantage of a regular working week are among the material benefits attached to a career in the GLS.

The work of a GLS lawyer actually matters, sometimes to everyone in the country. It is the importance and variety of the work of the GLS which more than anything sets it apart from any other part of the legal profession. Whether you are seeking a new direction for your career or have yet to enter the legal profession, you owe it to yourself to find out more about this unusual and interesting alternative to the private sector.

More information about the GLS and its work can be obtained from the GLS Recruitment Team, Queen Anne's Chambers, 28 Broadway, London SW1H 9JS. Tel: 071-210 3304.

The Crown Prosecution Service
GRAEME McKERRELL

Graeme McKerrell qualified as a solicitor in 1985 having been articled in private practice and began his prosecuting career with the Sussex Police Authority. When the CPS began operating in 1986 he was appointed as a Crown Prosecutor based in Chichester. He remained in the Sussex area and gained promotion to Senior Crown Prosecutor and then Principal Crown Prosecutor before taking up his present position as Head of Recruitment in April 1991.

General background

The Crown Prosecution Service (CPS) was launched in October 1986 and has already had a great impact on the criminal justice system. This is not surprising, since it is responsible for the conduct of all the criminal proceedings instituted by the police throughout England and Wales (with the exception of some minor offences).

Before 1986, the system had tended to work on a solicitor and client basis, with the police as the client. The Prosecution of Offences Act 1985 removed that relationship and established the independence of the CPS. It provided for the appointment of qualified barristers and solicitors as Crown Prosecutors, who are required to review the matter referred to them and decide whether or not a case should be prosecuted. Thus, once the police have completed their investigations and laid charges, CPS staff have to decide whether the case should proceed, to conduct the prosecution in the magistrates' court, and to brief counsel if the case goes on to the crown court.

The structure of the CPS

The Director of Public Prosecutions is head of the CPS and is situated at the Service's headquarters in London.

The CPS employs nearly 2,000 lawyers (more than any other organization) and 3,700 law clerks and administrative staff. There are over 100 offices grouped into thirty-one areas throughout England and Wales. The CPS has a Chief Executive and Deputy Director and each one of the thirty-one areas has a Chief Crown Prosecutor. The DPP on behalf of the Service is answerable to the Attorney General who is the government minister responsible for the CPS.

Career opportunities

Both barristers and solicitors can work as lawyers in the CPS. Lawyers with limited or even no previous experience join in the grade of Crown Prosecutor. They receive training in the work of the CPS and spend much of their time prosecuting whole lists of cases in magistrates' courts. In this way they rapidly gain extensive experience of advocacy and criminal litigation. They also review cases, under the guidance of their more senior colleagues, to decide which should proceed, and they advise police officers on the merits of particular cases.

After two years' satisfactory service there is the opportunity to be regraded to Senior Crown Prosecutor. Lawyers with three or four years' relevant experience can be appointed directly as a Senior Crown Prosecutor. Further opportunities exist for particularly able lawyers to advance to the grade of Principal Crown Prosecutor. Principal Crown Prosecutors still regularly go to court but tend to concentrate on the more difficult and complex cases. They also guide and supervise their prosecutors and prepare them for wider responsibilities.

It is possible for lawyers to specialize in particular fields, such as juvenile work or fraud cases. They can also seek promotion to Branch Crown Prosecutor. Branch Crown Prosecutors are lawyers responsible for a complete office or small group of offices. They still go to court, but are primarily managers of both the lawyers and the support staff in the office, who will include law clerks in a crown court section responsible for briefing counsel. Branch Crown Prosecutors report to the Chief Crown Prosecutor for the area. If management responsibilities do not appeal, promotion to Special Casework Lawyer is possible. These lawyers deal with the most complex or serious cases in their area.

Lawyers in the Service can remain in one office throughout their career. Often, however, they can increase their prospects of promotion, and gain wider experience, by moving between offices. Financial assistance is provided if this means moving house.

The Crown Prosecution Service therefore offers all lawyers the opportunity both to gain experience in all aspects of prosecution work and to rise to the most senior positions in the civil service.

Pupil barristers and trainee solicitors in CPS

The CPS has two hundred places for both barristers who wish to undertake pupillage and for trainee solicitors wishing to become solicitors, where great emphasis is placed on ensuring that a thorough training is given.

'You will now retire and consider your verdicts.'

The lawyer in local government
HELMUT CARTWRIGHT

Helmut Cartwright graduated from Oxford in 1966. Having been articled with a county council he worked for two others before becoming the County Secretary and Solicitor to East Sussex County Council in 1988. He is one of the Joint National Coordinators of the Lawyers in Local Government Careers Promotion Initiative. There are nineteen solicitors and one trainee solicitor in his department working with legal executives and other staff. The department provides legal services and advice, as well as a range of administrative and support services akin to many company secretarial functions in a large organization.

What are you looking for?

Is it challenge, helping things happen, working with and for people, helping individuals and colleagues to achieve what they otherwise would not, contributing to your community, seeing the results, the opportunity for training and development, finding solutions to complex problems, variety, excitement, sense of purpose, public service and job satisfaction – not to mention competitive salaries during training?

Local government offers each and every one of these and more besides.

What is local government about?

Local government is elected independently from central government and is part of our system of government.

Local government is about improving the quality of life, developing many policies and programmes to suit local needs and population structure, providing quality services, customer care, better information to, and involvement of, the public in service provision, greater choice wherever possible, value for money, protecting the environment, developing new relationships and methods of operation to meet the changing statutory framework and changing local circumstances, as well as prioritizing what can be achieved. Local councils do this in three main ways:

- by providing a wide range of services within their statutory powers

which are essential to their area and communities. Services can be provided through their own staff who may have had to successfully compete for the work, or through a range of contractual or other arrangements with private individuals or contractors, voluntary bodies or other agencies, eg health authorities or other local authorities. It will usually also involve investing in infrastructure such as schools, libraries, roads, leisure facilities and a whole range of other facilities
- by a wide range of statutory regulatory powers, particularly those protecting our environment
- by acting as local government in planning strategically and speaking out for, and promoting, their areas, acting as a local catalyst in bringing people/firms/interests/groups/local authorities and other agencies together to enable things to happen which would not otherwise have occurred and, generally, using their influence for the benefit of their area.

As an example, East Sussex, by no means one of the largest local authorities, has some 22,000 employees including teachers, social workers, engineers, planners, architects and property personnel, information technology specialists, librarians, accountants and a range of staff in direct service organizations established to compete under the competitive tendering legislation. The county council spends about a million pounds a day on services for the people of East Sussex, as well as speaking up for East Sussex.

What is the lawyers' challenge?

Councils derive all their functions, duties and powers from statutes. Recent legislation is extremely complex and the pace of change shows no sign of slowing down. Many of the changes are major new departures, major changes in responsibilities and relationships, not to mention changes in methods of delivery. Resources are limited, so questions of priority are important.

Council policies, practice and methods of operation have been changing and evolving to comply with the law: lawyers' advice to their councils, individual councillors and other departments are a key part of that process.

How does our policy need to change, what is the effect of that on council priorities, resources, can the council still achieve what it wants, if so how, and how does it make things happen? These are just some of the questions lawyers handle. The long awaited Children's Act which came into effect in October

1991 is an example. It is the most major change in approach to the rights of children and parents for more than fifty years. For that Act, as in other cases, lawyers were involved in training others as well as being trained themselves: they need to be able to both advise their social services colleagues and other specialists involved, as well as knowing the new court processes. Care in the community, changes in education, housing: I could go on.

The lawyers' challenge is to find solutions which will enable their council's policies to develop and to help colleagues to achieve them and provide quality services at an affordable cost.

Lawyers in local government provide both corporate legal advice and legal services. The need for both and their relevance in determining priorities and achieving objectives remains as ever. The range, interest, variety and challenge of the work is enormous.

Public expectations have never been higher. Many of the new statutory duties incorporate clearer remedies and rights of redress and the incidence of legal challenge by judicial review seems to be increasing. Standards of performance and customer care go to the heart of the concept of 'Citizen's Charters'. Change is both challenge and opportunity.

What of the future?

There are 449 separate and independent local authorities in England and Wales, which together with a small number of statutory joint bodies are responsible for the provision of their communities of a range of important services. The principal services are: housing; education; social services; countryside amenities; recreation; libraries; museums; arts; police; fire-rescue; consumer protection; environmental health; highways and traffic; public transport; waste collection and disposal; planning and economic development.

In the seven Metropolitan areas of Greater London, West Midlands, Greater Manchester, Merseyside, South Yorkshire, West Yorkshire and Tyne & Wear, a single tier of local authorities, the thirty-three London borough councils and the thirty-five Metropolitan district councils, together with some joint bodies of those councils are responsible for all these services. In the rest of the country there is a two-tier structure of forty-seven county councils and 333 shire district councils supported in most areas by parish, town or community councils. The services are provided in most cases by either county or district councils, but in respect of some services responsibility is split or shared.

Most, but not all, local authorities have an 'in-house' legal service. However, not all recruit trainee solicitors: of those that do, few recruit more than one a year and many only one every other year. In all, local authorities seek to appoint about 150 trainees for each year, some two years ahead of appointment, others one year ahead, but the majority only shortly before appointment. Councils advertise individually. Vacancies will usually be notified direct to careers advisory services and/or advertised in the *Law Society Gazette* and the spring and autumn special student editions of the *Lawyer*.

The size of legal departments and the range of work undertaken vary considerably but are principally dictated by the following factors:

- the functions for which the authority is responsible;
- the size of the population it serves; and
- the degree to which work is as a matter of policy contracted out to the private sector.

Broadly speaking, county councils, London borough councils and Metropolitan councils have the broadest range of functions, serve the largest populations and will, therefore, have the larger legal departments. However, there are also some Shire district councils serving large populations with, in consequence, large legal departments, and all local authorities recruiting trainee solicitors can offer the range and quality of experience necessary to satisfy not merely Law Society requirements but also the intellectual demands and interest of the most demanding individual.

Litigation, advocacy, intellectual property, employment, trusts, company law, building and development agreements, property/commercial property are all part of the legal advice and services covered in most departments.

However local government may be organized in the future, services will still be needed however they may be provided. While there is local government there will be a need for lawyers in local government.

Are we so very different?

Perhaps the first thing to stress is that we solicitors are all in one single profession with a common legal training. It is the similarities between our work rather than the differences which stand out. Even during articles it is only the working environment that is different. Movement between private sector and local government is becoming increasingly common early on in the professional career to the actual benefit of both sectors.

For those who wish to make the move into the private sector, the quality of local government professionals make them a much sought after and valued commodity. We in local government for our part appreciate the sometimes different approach that is brought to bear on our organizations and problems by those of our private practice colleagues who join us. If legal services in local government becomes subject to compulsory competitive tendering in due course, our similarity in operation is likely to increase.

The main difference is, of course, that we have but one client, our council, with no need or indeed right to seek other clients elsewhere. In this respect we do, of course, have much in common with our commerce and industry group colleagues. In both these sectors the importance of the 'in-house lawyer' with an understanding of the client's organization and the background to problems that arise is recognized. The ability to participate in the formulation of policies and the working out of decisions means that many a potential legal difficulty, if not disaster, is averted at the outset, an opportunity much less frequently open to our private practice colleagues.

The choice is yours

In my personal view the career prospects for the able local government lawyer are better today than they ever have been. There is no shortage of challenging legal problems awaiting solution. The local government lawyer has a career which offers:

At all stages

- Personal responsibility but with guidance appropriate to experience and ability
- Challenging problems requiring practical solutions
- A political and corporate environment in a wide range of authorities
- The attraction of multidisciplinary working
- Flexible working conditions particularly attractive to those wishing to take up the law at any stage or return to work either full-time or part-time
- Equal opportunities for all.

During training

- Broad range of work related to the services that the authority provides

and satisfying Law Society requirements
- A competitive salary
- Opportunities for advocacy not available to colleagues in other sectors
- Possibility of part-time training.

After admission

- Professional development through management training and continuing professional education
- A wide range of high-quality work
- Opportunity to specialize
- Service to the local community including voluntary and business sectors
- Long-term prospects with scope for progressing into legal and general management
- Experience valued by private practice
- Openings for those trained and experienced in other sectors.

Further enquiries

If you would like to find out more about a legal career in local government before making your decision:

(a) Ask your careers service adviser for a copy of our careers brochure 'More than just a Career', and for our vacancy brochure.

(b) See also our ten minute video 'More than just a Career' which the careers service will have in their resource centre.

(c) Visit the 'Lawyers in Local Government' stand at major careers fairs.

(d) Ask your careers service adviser to put you in touch with one of our liaison officers.

(e) Get in touch with your local council's solicitor who will be pleased to talk to you and may be able to offer work experience.

(f) Write or phone the Careers Promotion and Recruitment Coordinators and they will do their best to advise you (please quote reference IG):

Jacqui Dixon, ADS National Recruitment Coordinator, Basingstoke & Deane Borough Council, Civic Offices, London Road, Basingstoke, Hampshire RG21 2AJ. Tel: 0256-844719. Helmut Cartwright, SOCS National Recruitment Coordinator, East Sussex County Council, Pelham House, St Andrew's Lane, Lewes, East Sussex BN7 1UN. Tel: 0273-481556.

The Magistrates' Courts Service
STEPHEN CAVEN

Stephen Caven graduated in law in 1978. Having obtained articles with a medium sized legal practice in Greater Manchester he remained with the firm after qualifying, eventually managing a branch office. In 1986, he 'stepped off the conveyancing treadmill' and embarked on a career as a court clerk in the Magistrates' Courts Service. He is now Deputy Clerk to the Middleton, Heywood and Rochdale Justices.

General background

Magistrates have played an important role in the administration of justice for more than six centuries. There are currently some 28,000 lay magistrates recruited from all walks of life. They are advised on matters of law and legal procedure by court clerks. There are currently over 2,000 court clerks. A large proportion of court clerks are professionally qualified as either solicitors or barristers.

Because magistrates have been part of the fabric of the legal system for so long, much of the associated terminology and nomenclature has an archaic or anachronistic flavour. For example, magistrates are also known as justices of the peace. They are appointed to one of the fifty-eight commission areas (outside London these are essentially counties). Within a commission area they are assigned to a bench which covers one of the 500 or so Petty Sessional Divisions (which are the catchment areas for court business). Their legal advisers are known as clerks despite the fact that many of them are solicitors or barristers of many years' standing.

This outdated appearance is, however, deceptive. Magistrates, advised by their clerks, are called upon to make judicial decisions involving a staggering variety of contemporary issues, reflecting the increasingly complex nature of modern society. Matters within their jurisdiction range from determining whether a child should be taken from its parents and placed in the care of the local authority because of alleged abuse, to deciding whether a new casino should be licensed.

The work of the courts

Every person charged with a criminal offence, however serious or sophisticated, must appear initially before a magistrates' court. The vast majority (around ninety-five per cent) of all criminal prosecutions are concluded there. Justices are empowered to determine finally, in appropriate cases, allegations such as burglary or the possession of controlled drugs. They also deal with matters which can only proceed at summary level including driving with excess alcohol or speeding. As regards the most serious offences such as murder or rape, magistrates will decide whether the accused is to be granted bail, and they may be required to decide in committal proceedings, if sufficient evidence has been adduced to justify the continuation of the trial before a jury at the Crown Court.

It is a common misconception that magistrates' courts are solely concerned with criminal proceedings. In fact magistrates have a wide ranging civil jurisdiction. They have the primary responsibility for the licensing of premises where alcohol is sold, from the corner off-licence to the most exclusive

'She did a year at RADA after graduating.'

restaurant. Their jurisdiction also encompasses the licensing of betting and gaming.

Justices have always had a central role in proceedings relating to children. Following the implementation of the Children Act 1989 this role has been further expanded. In the area of private law, dealing with the resolution of disputes between individuals over the upbringing of children, magistrates have been given, in many cases, concurrent jurisdiction with the higher courts.

Proceedings in the field of public law, concerned with the intervention of the state to protect children at risk, are almost invariably commenced in magistrates' courts. A great deal of understanding and expertise on the part of justices and their legal advisers is required in responding to the sensitive issues raised by such proceedings.

A career as a court clerk

Magistrates are essentially lay persons who serve on their local bench on a voluntary basis. In an era of increasingly complex legislation they rely to a great extent on their legal adviser, the court clerk, for guidance on questions of law. Most courts have a team of court clerks grouped under the clerk to the justices, who has the overall responsibility for the smooth running of the court.

There is a growing emphasis on managing resources efficiently and making the best use of technological advances in the courts' service. Effective management and administration are essential. But the primary duty of the clerk to the justices has always been to provide legal advice to justices. On a day-to-day basis this function will be discharged by court clerks who have the responsibility for all matters listed in a particular court.

A large number of court clerks are solicitors or barristers and in order to be appointed as a clerk to the justices it is necessary to be a solicitor or barrister of five years' standing. It is possible to become a court clerk by obtaining a Diploma in Magisterial Law, which requires attendance on a two-year part-time course whilst employed in the courts' service. However, most courts recognize the value of professionally qualified court clerks and actively seek to recruit recently qualified solicitors or barristers. For those working in the courts sponsorship is usually available to candidates for the Law Society or Bar Finals. Articles of clerkship are normally available although court clerks with five years' experience are exempt from the requirement to serve articles before admission.

The diverse nature of proceedings in magistrates' courts means that the work of a court clerk is usually stimulating and interesting. There are opportunities to develop expertise in a wide variety of legal fields. In addition, clerks with the ability to explain legal principles in a clear and concise manner are in great demand for the continuing programme of magistrates' training. The large number of courts in England and Wales provide a wide range of alternative options, both in terms of geographical area and the size of court. Whether it be in a busy urban environment or a small rural courthouse, the Magistrates' Courts Service offers the possibility of a challenging and rewarding career.

Working at a law centre
MELODY PAVEY

Melody Pavey is a Policy and Research Officer at the Law Centres Federation, having previously worked in a South London Law Centre. Her ten years' experience enables her to give a valuable insight into this important part of our legal structure.

In the UK, sixty law centres (LCs) advise and represent people and groups within their locality. Most law centres receive a grant from their local authorities for salaries and running costs. A very few are financed from central government via the Lord Chancellor's Legal Aid Board. They are run by management committees, made up of consumers and community representatives, who also decide on the general direction of the law centre. In this way, law centres aim to tailor their service to the needs of the community.

The role

The remit of a law centre is to provide legal support to those with most need. The order of priorities within this broad aim is usually fine-tuned by the management committee, but the areas which always figure are housing in the rented sector, employment in relation to the rights of the employee at work, immigration and nationality; welfare rights and benefits; children's rights in respect of education, care and wardship and in a few cases, crime. However, they are not limited to these areas of law. In fact an important function of law centres is to make the benefits of new legislation accessible to their clients. For example, recent developments include working to ensure that rights under environmental and European legislation can be enforced.

Given their role and the need to target their limited resources, LCs do not handle adult crime, conveyancing, probate, divorce or commercial work, as these are covered by the private sector.

Careers in a law centre

To be allowed to operate, a LC has to employ at least one solicitor of three or more years' post-qualification experience. Barristers can also be employed and indeed this is the only salaried work permitted to a practising member of the Bar. A law centre needs to incorporate a wide range of skills, including representing clients in court, in front of tribunals and in negotiations with other bodies. In addition to their legally qualified staff, most centres employ specialist advice and community workers, as many problems have more than just a legal dimension.

Working in this environment you will need to talk to clients sympathetically, encouraging and assisting them to deal with as much of their problems themselves. You work with community groups, giving talks and writing leaflets that demystify the law and make it accessible to all members of the community.

LCs are able, so long as they satisfy the Law Society rules, to take on articled clerks. This is still a relatively rare occurrence, if only because resources are stretched and no systematic scheme exists at present.

The Law Centres Federation

The umbrella body representing all LCs is the Law Centres Federation, which helps in the development of the services and structure of existing LCs and in the expansion of the national network. In addition, it publicizes the work of the LCs, acts as a conduit to government based on experience gained by its members, so influencing both existing policy and forthcoming legislation, and continues the ceaseless campaign for secure funding.

Further information is available by writing to The Law Centres Federation, Duchess House, 18-19 Warren Street, London W1P 5DB. Tel: 071-387 8570.

Transferring from the Law Society to the Bar

Every year, just as a number of barristers decide that they would prefer, for a whole range of reasons, to become solicitors, so every year a similar impulse causes a number of solicitors to apply to transfer to the Bar. 'Qualified legal practitioners', with experience, usually receive a favourable hearing as the Bar Council values the experience they bring.

In practical terms, at present, the procedure for transfer is as follows (though the European Directive to allow in EC lawyers might result in some changes in the near future): The solicitor is asked by the Joint Regulations Committee to obtain two certificates of good character, one usually from the employer/senior partner and one from a member of the Council of the Law Society or someone of similar standing. A certificate of qualification as a solicitor is also required, as is evidence that the applicant intends to take up practice at the Bar. The applicant is asked to join an Inn and complete four dining terms before being called to the Bar. No admission is possible before the solicitor's name has been removed from the Law Society's Roll.

A former solicitor is not usually required to pass any of the examinations in the core subjects, or any section of the Bar Examination except Sections III (civil and criminal procedure) and IV (evidence). The Joint Regulations Committee has discretion to grant exemption from these and from the practical exercises and this discretion is exercised where sufficient experience and expertise is apparent in the candidate. Pupillage may be deemed inappropriate but this exemption is again dependent on individual cases and may in future depend to a greater extent on advocacy experience.

Given the existence of two branches to the legal profession, it is desirable for a mechanism to exist that allows lawyers to redirect their career. Both branches benefit and this flexibility ensures that valuable practitioners, who might otherwise leave, remain in the profession.

Copies of the full regulations in this area can be obtained from the Inns of Court School of Law, 4 Gray's Inn Place, London WC1R 5DX. Tel: 071-404 5787.

Information and statistics

Introduction

The information and statistics set out in this chapter and the one in part III are extracts from the Annual Statistical Report of the Law Society. The report was compiled by Stephen Harwood of the Law Society's Research and Policy Planning Unit who has produced quite the most comprehensive analysis of the profession available to date. What follows here can only be a subjective selection and for a fuller and thus more accurate picture, it is recommended that a copy of the report is purchased at £14.50 from Chancery Lane.

Routes of admission to the Roll

There are now eight routes to qualification as a solicitor, which are:

(a) Law graduate
(b) Non-law graduate
(c) Mature student
(d) Overseas lawyer (transfer)
(e) Barrister (transfer)
(f) Scottish/Northern Irish lawyers (transfer)
(g) Fellow of the Institute of Legal Executives
(h) Justices' clerk

The shortest route to qualification is by law degree, where training can be completed in three years after obtaining a degree. The vast majority of entrants to the profession choose this route, with 2,766 (sixty-five per cent) of those admitted in 1990–91 being law graduates. Non-law graduates have to undertake a conversion course, the Common Professional Examination (CPE), which can be completed in a year. They then proceed to qualify in the same way as a law graduate. This is the second most popular direct route to admission, with 411 (ten per cent) qualifying by this route in 1990–91. The proportion qualifying by this route has remained relatively stable over the past few years. In 1990–91, therefore, seventy-five per cent of all newly admitted solicitors qualified by virtue of being a graduate. The supply of graduates is therefore a crucial factor influencing the supply of recruits to the profession.

Mature students (over twenty-five with no degree) can also enter the profession. School-leavers can also qualify direct from school until 1994. They have to pass the Solicitors' First Examination in addition to the Final Examination and undertake five-year articles, or four-year articles plus one year on a recognized course for the Final Examination. The Solicitors' First Examination is to be abolished by the Law Society Training Regulations 1990. Mature students must pass an eight-subject CPE which takes two years (the CPE has six subjects for non-law graduates), pass the Final Examination and complete two-year articles. The numbers qualifying by these routes is very low and in 1990–91 just four mature students qualified to become solicitors. By far the most important route for qualification for mature students and school-leavers is now via transfer after obtaining qualification as a Fellow of the Institute of Legal Executives (FILEX) and passing the Solicitors' Final Examinations.

The other routes to admission are by transfer from other legal professions to the solicitors' profession. Although in the past relatively small numbers of barristers, overseas lawyers and Scottish and Northern Irish lawyers were admitted to the profession each year, there has been a large increase in their numbers in the past two years. In 1990–91, four per cent of those admitted

Route to admission of solicitors admitted to the Roll in the years to 31st July 1990 and 1991

Route	*Year to 31/7/90*	*Year to 31/7/91*
Law graduate	2,508 (67.3%)	2,766 (64.9%)
Non-law graduate	549 (14.7%)	411 (9.6%)
School leaver	1 (0.0%)	– –
Mature student	1 (0.0%)	4 (0.1%)
Overseas lawyer	388 (10.4%)	565 (13.3%)
Barrister	129 (3.5%)	185 (4.3%)
Scot/Northern Ireland lawyers	63 (1.7%)	212 (5.0%)
FILEX (Legal executives)	53 (1.4%)	82 (1.9%)
Justices' clerk	37 (1.0%)	40 (0.9%)
Total	**3,729 (100%)**	**4,265 (100%)**

were barristers, thirteen per cent were overseas lawyers and a further five per cent were either Scottish or Northern Irish lawyers. Not all overseas lawyers are eligible for admission to the solicitors' profession in England and Wales under the Transfer Regulations. A detailed breakdown of those admitted is presented on page 121.

Graduates

In the year 1st August 1990 to 31st July 1991, of 4,265 admitted to the Roll of Solicitors, sixty-five per cent were by direct qualification as law graduates and a further ten per cent as non-law graduates, giving a total direct graduate entry of seventy-five per cent.

The table below shows the numbers of university and polytechnic graduates for each of the last five years.

Numbers of law graduates 1986–1990

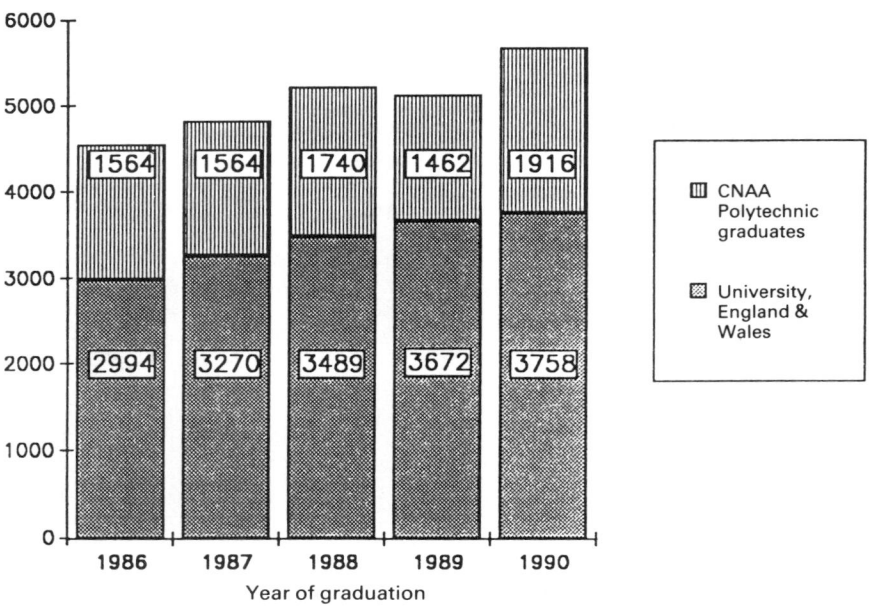

Solicitors' Final Examination

The Law Society's Final is an exam which, with very few exceptions, must be passed to achieve qualification as a solicitor. The course lasts for one academic year. The table below shows the number of places being offered by the recognized institutions that conduct the course. The last Finals course will commence in September 1992, and the last full sitting will take place in July 1993. The College of Law will be providing additional places on an evening course in 1991–92 in order to help meet demand for places. The scheme was introduced last year. The Polytechnic of Wales will also be offering the course for the first time in the academic year 1991–92.

Places on the Solicitors' Final Examination course for 1989–90, 1990–91 and the planned intake for 1991–92

	1989–90	1990–91	1991–92
Birmingham Polytechnic	130	120	120
Bristol Polytechnic	160	200	200
City of London Polytechnic	100	100	120
The College of Law –			
London, Chancery Lane	336	425)	
London, Lancaster Gate	430	550)	
Guildford	954	1,000	4,089*
Chester	1,010	1,218)	
York	500	770)	
Leeds Polytechnic	100	100	200
Leicester Polytechnic	–	80	130
Manchester Polytechnic	150	175	175
Newcastle-upon-Tyne Polytechnic	100	110	135
Trent Polytechnic (Nottingham)	125	125	150
Polytechnic of Wales	–	–	90
Wolverhampton Polytechnic	75	75	120
Total places	**4,170**	**5,048**	**5,529**

* Due to new 'clearing house' admissions it has not been possible to obtain the breakdown of places by each branch of the College of Law for 1991–92

Statistics on the results of the Final Examinations have in the past been published in the Law Society's Gazette. The table below provides a summary of these statistics. Not only are the number of women attempting the Solicitors' Finals on the increase, but women are continually achieving a much higher pass rate than men.

Results of first time candidates attempting the summer Solicitors' Final Examinations 1985 to 1990

Year	Candidates sitting the Final Examination			Numbers and (percentages) passing the Final Examination		
	Men	Women	Total	Men	Women	Total
1985	1,757	1,479	3,236	961 (54.6%)	908 (61.4%)	1,869 (57.8%)
1986	1,667	1,575	3,242	902 (54.1%)	1,046 (66.4%)	1,948 (60.1%)
1987	1,615	1,620	3,235	959 (59.4%)	1,100 (67.9%)	2,059 (63.6%)
1988	1,654	1,662	3,316	1,145 (69.2%)	1,234 (74.2%)	2,379 (71.7%)
1989	1,704	1,841	3,545	1,204 (70.7%)	1,379 (74.9%)	2,583 (72.9%)
1990	1,965	2,155	4,120	1,488 (75.7%)	1,682 (78.1%)	3,170 (76.9%)

Articles registered

As part of a solicitor's training, a trainee solicitor is required to work in a solicitor's office in order to gain experience in the work undertaken by solicitors. These periods of training are called 'articles' and the student is described as being 'articled' to a particular solicitor, the 'principal', who is responsible for his or her training.

There were 3,842 new articles registered in the year 1st August 1990 to 31st July 1991. This represents an increase of eighteen per cent on the 3,254 new articles registered in the previous year. The proportion of new articles registered by women was fifty-four per cent, an increase on the fifty-two per cent of new articles registered by women last year. This lends further support to there being growing numbers of women in the profession in the future.

New articles entered into between 1st August and 31st July 1989–90 and 1990–91

Region	New articles 1989–90			New articles 1990–91			
	Men	Women	Total	Men	Women	Unknown*	Total
North	278	295	573	306	338	1	644
Midlands	166	178	344	172	241	1	413
Wales	64	69	133	54	82	–	136
South West	85	87	172	79	116	–	185
South East	165	231	396	172	287	1	459
Outer London	116	140	256	135	168	–	303
Central London	680	688	1,369	837	820	–	1,657
Not known*	5	7	11	15	17	–	32
Total	**1,559**	**1,695**	**3,254**	**1,770**	**2,069**	**3**	**3,842**

* Location of articles was omitted in 11 cases in 1989–90 and 32 cases in 1990–91. Sex was not identified in 3 cases in 1990–91

The table below shows the average 1990–91 starting salaries of trainee solicitors entering articles. The percentage of clerks on the national minimum salary laid down by the Law Society is also shown. In all regions, the proportion on the minimum starting salary increased marginally on the previous year.

National minimum starting salaries for trainee solicitors

Effective date	Provinces	Outer London	Inner London
From 1/8/87	£5,200	£6,100	£6,600
From 1/8/88	£6,000	£6,900	£7,200
From 1/8/89	£7,300	£8,200	£8,500
From 1/8/90	£8,700	£9,600	£9,900
From 1/8/91	£10,100	£11,000	£11,300

The table overleaf shows the average 1990–91 starting salaries of trainee solicitors entering articles. The percentage of clerks on the national minimum salary laid down by the Law Society is also shown.

Average starting salaries of trainee solicitors 1990–91

Region	Average salary	Percentage on minimum salary	Number of cases
North	£9,999	27.8%	645
Midlands	£10,629	17.1%	414
Wales	£9,411	46.3%	136
South West	£9,941	13.3%	195
South East	£10,506	9.6%	460
Outer London	£12,083	13.2%	303
Inner London	£16,115	0.4%	1,657
All regions	£12,931	11.3%	3,810

Admissions to the Roll

The number of people admitted to the Roll of Solicitors in England and Wales in the year 1st August 1990 to 31st July 1991 was 4,265. This was the largest number of solicitors ever admitted in any one year and represents an increase of 14.4 per cent on the 3,729 admitted last year.

The table below provides a breakdown of the sex of solicitors admitted in recent years.

Numbers of solicitors admitted to the Roll

Year	Men	Per cent	Women	Per cent	Total
1985	1,572	58.6%	1,111	41.4%	2,683
1986	1,524	55.9%	1,201	44.1%	2,725
1987	1,626	54.7%	1,347	45.3%	2,973
1988	1,750	53.9%	1,494	46.1%	3,244
1988–89*	1,834	53.4%	1,600	46.6%	3,434
1989–90	1,990	53.4%	1,739	46.6%	3,729
1990–91	2,238	52.5%	2,027	47.5%	4,265

* Date of recording changed to year 1st August to 31st July from 1988–89 onwards

Part V
Becoming a barrister

What does a barrister do?

What makes a barrister different from a solicitor? What does he spend his time doing? The answer depends partly on his type of practice. It might be a purely criminal practice where he will both prosecute and defend people in the crown court and magistrates' courts, or it might be that he specializes in shipping law or patents or libel. However, broadly speaking, he or she may provide two things: an expert opinion, or powers of persuasion.

Unlike solicitors, the barrister has no direct contact with the public. He accepts his instructions to advise or act on a client's behalf through a solicitor. Recently, the Bar has changed its Code of Conduct to allow other professions to brief barristers on behalf of their clients in certain cases, but there is still no daily contact with the client in the way that the solicitor has. The reason for this lies not in any sense of exclusiveness, but in the different roles which each of these lawyers is designed to play.

The division of role, and often work, between the professions is much like that of GP and consultant. Solicitor and barrister are both lawyers, but each has different and complementary skills. The solicitor, like the GP, is the first point of contact for the public. He interviews his clients and finds out what their particular problem is. He collects all the evidence surrounding the matter which might be useful, taking notes and arranging for clarification of anything outstanding so that he can build up an accurate picture of the whole matter. If it can then be easily resolved, he will handle it himself. If it cannot be, or is otherwise complicated, he will want a second opinion from a specialist as to the likely consequences.

This is where the barrister comes in. He will often receive instructions in the form of 'counsel to advise', where he will refine the points in issue presented by the solicitor or other professional and map out the way the courts would currently be likely to decide them. At the next stage, he might be asked to draft the pleadings – to draw up the precise allegations of fact which are to be presented before the court, or to draft the other formal documents and affidavits which are necessary for court proceedings. Finally, he will go into the court himself and present the case, for which he is particularly trained.

This means that, in practice, the barrister divides his time between advising on problems in writing and in conferences (ie meetings between barrister, solicitor/other professional and client), and taking the matter further by moulding it into a case, ready for presentation in court, and then appearing on his client's behalf to argue it.

Once in court, his particular skills as an advocate, which are developed by regular appearances and which depend on regular practice, come into play. Here he presents and analyses facts, adduces evidence by oral examination and cross-examination of witnesses, and argues law.

It is on this basis that barristers have to date been accorded the sole right of audience (ie the ability to present cases) in the higher courts in our legal system.

All these tasks mean that the barrister's professional life involves irregular and often long hours and also a great deal of time travelling and waiting around at court. Work will often come in concentrated doses. Instructions may be received minutes rather than days before a hearing.

So, what are the qualities that distinguish a barrister?

- He or she must have the intellectual qualities which any good lawyer needs.
- A barrister must have physical and mental stamina.
- A barrister must enjoy solving problems.
- A barrister must be able to communicate effectively with all sorts of people and enjoy doing so. He will be expected to deal with people from all walks of life, some articulate, some not, some intelligent, others less so.
- A barrister needs a highly enquiring mind, one that is curious about all things – cases have been won because the advocate happened to have some piece of general or specialist knowledge at the back of his mind which he was able to draw out at the crucial moment.
- He or she must be someone who can cope with the insecurity and uncertainty of being self-employed in a highly competitive profession.

The reward, when success comes, is a sense of personal achievement and self-fulfilment that is hard to match. The Bar is competitive – you pitch your skills daily against other men and women in the courts and live or die by your reputation as an advocate – but it is also highly supportive and friendly. And like other practising lawyers, you are constantly reminded that your work has a genuine and useful bearing on the lives of your clients.

Routes into the profession
SUSAN BLAKE

Susan Blake LLM, MA, was called to the Bar in 1976 and is now Reader in Law at the Council of Legal Education. She is the Course Director of the Vocational Course and played a substantial role in its development.

In this article reference will be made to the Council of Legal Education which operates as the governing body of the Inns of Court School of Law and is responsible for the conduct of the Bar Examination and for the Assessment process on the Vocational Course, and to the Inns of Court School of Law (ICSL) which provides the teaching for the Vocational Course but not for the Bar Examination. The address of both bodies is: 4 Gray's Inn Place, London WC1R 5DX. Tel: 071-404 5787.

How can I judge if the Bar is for me?

Before choosing a career in law and/or deciding on which branch of the legal profession to join, it is advisable to spend time in a set of chambers. Many sets offer 'mini-pupillages'. These provide an ideal opportunity to experience first hand the full range of work which the Bar does and to soak up the atmosphere of the life style of the barrister. Time invested in a mini-pupillage will help you to know whether the Bar is for you – to know whether you have the determination to succeed in a profession where self-confidence is crucial and where the ability to manage yourself and your time very efficiently is an absolute necessity. If you need someone behind you to tell you what to do and when to do it – or if you are shy of hard work – the Bar is not for you. Barristers are self-motivated and self-starting – you must know yourself and whether you are the kind of person who can cope with this life style.

For information about how to obtain a mini-pupillage contact the General Council of the Bar or the student officer of any of the four Inns of Court.

Vocational training

The only route to qualification for those intending to enter pupillage, to obtain a practising certificate and to become a practising barrister in the territory of any member state of the European Community, is through the successful completion of the Vocational Course. This course is only available at the Inns of Court School of Law.

The Bar Examination is held for those who wish to be called to the Bar of England and Wales but who do not intend to practise as a barrister in any member state of the European Community and for those who, having sat the Bar Examination already, have yet to be successful in it. (Transitional arrangements will operate for a time to enable those who were partly qualified as at Michaelmas 1989 under the Bar Examination system to complete their training and then to practise as a barrister.)

Who is qualified for entry onto the Vocational Course at the Inns of Court School of Law (ICSL)?

Those who are members of one of the four Inns of Court *and* who have successfully completed the 'academic stage' of their training *and* intend to practise as a barrister in any member state of the European Community are entitled to enrol on the Vocational Course. It is important to realize that anyone who intends to practise as a barrister in any member state of the European Community, whether immediately or in the future, must successfully complete the Vocational Course at the ICSL. Plans are being discussed for the introduction of a selection scheme for the Vocational Course from 1993, and it is possible that a limited form of selection will be introduced before that date, due to an increased demand for places at the ICSL. Students should make enquiries early in the academic year prior to that in which they hope to attend ICSL.

The 'academic stage' of training can be completed in the following ways:

Law graduates

Law graduates can qualify for entry onto the Vocational Course or to take the Bar Examination (for the latter, see below) by successfully completing, at the required standard, a 'qualifying law degree' in law or in law combined with other subjects. In either case the degree must include the so-called 'core legal subjects' (namely: the law of contract, criminal law, constitutional and administrative law, land law, the law of torts and equity and trusts) and, in each of these six subjects, a satisfactory level of attainment must have been achieved.

A 'qualifying law degree'
In order for a degree to be a 'qualifying' one it must have been granted by an institution situated in England and Wales and be approved for this purpose by the Council of Legal Education, and normally have been obtained within the last five years (for the rules which apply when a degree is more than five years old see the Consolidated Regulations available in the Calendar from the Council of Legal Education). A list of approved degrees is available from the Council of Legal Education.

The required standard of degree
This is normally that of lower second class or better. In cases where there were very exceptional circumstances which adversely affected the applicant's performance on his or her degree programme and hence the quality of the degree obtained, graduates with a third class degree, or a pass or unclassified degree, may be considered for entry. Each case is considered on its merits and enquiries should be made of the Assistant to the Dean, Inns of Court School of Law.

The 'core legal subjects'
It is recognized that the content of law degrees varies from institution to institution; some include the six 'core legal subjects' as a compulsory part of their degree course whilst others may offer these subjects as options. A student who wishes to become a barrister must study these subjects and, in general, it is often easier to study them as part of the degree. Institutions may use different titles to describe these subjects and sometimes parts of these subjects are taught in combination with other subjects. In most of these cases the Council of Legal Education will have agreed with the institution concerned that it will treat these subjects as the equivalent of the core legal subject(s). A graduate whose degree does not include in some form or other all six 'core legal subjects', or who has failed one or more of these subjects (whilst nevertheless achieving a satisfactory standard of degree overall) can make up the deficit in the Common Professional Examination. Information about the Common Professional Examination can be obtained from the Council of Legal Education.

Non-law graduates
Non-law graduates can qualify for admission by successfully completing, at the required standard, a degree in a subject or subjects other than law studied at a university, polytechnic or other institution in the United Kingdom or the Republic of Ireland, and successfully completing a one-year full time course leading to the Common Professional Examination.

The Common Professional Examination (CPE)
The course leading to the Common Professional Examination provides tuition in the 'core legal subjects' (detailed above) and gives sufficient grounding in the basic principles of law and legal method as necessary to enable non-law graduates to undertake the practical training on the Vocational Course. The CPE course is particularly intensive since students are required to study the 'core legal subjects' in the same depth as on a law degree course but over a very much shorter period of time than would traditionally be spent on these subjects on a law degree. Information about the CPE courses can be obtained from the Council of Legal Education.

The required standard of degree
Normally only those degrees which are obtained at a lower second class or better standard will entitle their holder to admission onto the Vocational Course, subject to the very exceptional circumstances explained above.

Will a non-law graduate suffer any disadvantage?
In a word, No! Many extremely successful members of the Bar and some of our most revered judges are graduates in disciplines other than law. In some specialist areas of practice being a graduate from another field is almost a prerequisite for success, for example at the Patent Bar many successful practitioners have science or engineering backgrounds. In any event, barristers often need to draw on their knowledge and understanding of business and commercial practices in order to find the most sensible solution to the lay client's particular problem – a broad educational or experiential background provides a foundation from which the practical solution can most easily be found.

Non-graduate mature students
These may qualify for admission if they have been accepted by an Inn of Court as having exceptional ability in an academic, professional, business

or administrative field and have successfully completed a full-time two-year course offered at the Polytechnic of Central London. (Further information can be obtained from the Eligibility Officer at the Inns of Court School of Law.)

The special course
This consists of the 'core legal subjects' (detailed above) and two other legal subjects which can be chosen from the list of subjects on offer. (Information about this course can be obtained from the Polytechnic of Central London.)

Graduates of overseas institutions

Graduates in law
These must first apply for a Certificate of Eligibility from the Council of Legal Education. This will specify the form of study and examination which must be undertaken in order to complete the academic stage of training. Generally, most graduates will be required to take some further examinations in the 'core legal subjects'.

Non-law graduates
Again these must first apply for a Certificate of Eligibility from the Council of Legal Education. This will specify the form of study and examination which must be undertaken in order to complete the academic stage of training. Such graduates must show a good knowledge of the English language and either show an intention to or have reasonable grounds to expect to practise at the Bar of England and Wales, or an intention to use the qualification in the course of a profession or employment in England and Wales, and have Home Office permission to remain in the UK to do so.

Those not intending to practise at the Bar of England and Wales

Those who do not intend to practise at the Bar of England and Wales and who are therefore usually not eligible to enrol on the Vocational Course but wish to be called to the Bar, must pass the Bar Examination. The syllabuses for the Bar Examination are published annually in the Calendar and for the time being the examination will continue in the same format. Any changes to the nature or format of this examination will be announced by the Council of Legal Education well in advance of the Trinity examination. Those who wish to qualify by this route must be members of one of the four Inns of Court and have successfully completed the 'academic stage of training' described fully above. The Inns of Court School of Law no longer offers a course to prepare candidates for this examination. However, courses are run by other institutions within the London area with whom the Council of Legal Education has made arrangements and the addresses of those institutions which offer such courses can be obtained from the Information Officer at the Council of Legal Education.

NB. Those from certain dependent territories may be entitled in limited circumstances to enrol on the Vocational Course provided that they can show an intention to practise in the legal profession of that territory.

Admission of qualified legal practitioners to the English Bar

Special provision is made for individuals who are already qualified as legal practitioners within the European Community. Such persons must apply to the Joint Regulations Committee of the Council of the Inns of Court and the General Council of the Bar, and they will be required to pass appropriate sections of the Aptitude Test which is administered twice a year by the Inns of Court School of Law. This test includes papers on core areas of English Law and on Evidence and Procedure, and oral assessments of advocacy skills and knowledge of professional conduct rules.

Pupillage

A person who intends to practise as a barrister is required to complete a twelve-month period in pupillage which is divided into the non-practising first six months and the practising second six months. It is for each individual to make their own arrangements for pupillage, but information is available as to pupillages offered. Information is best sought through student officers of any of the four Inns of Court. The ICSL can only give limited general advice on pupillage for those taking the Vocational Course.

The formal training – the Vocational Course and the Bar Examination

SUSAN BLAKE

Susan Blake LLM, MA, was called to the Bar in 1976 and is now Reader in Law at the Council of Legal Education. She is the Course Director of the Vocational Course and played a substantial role in its development.

There are two different arrangements governing the formal training to be called to the Bar of England and Wales. The choice of which training scheme to follow depends on an individual's future intentions as to the geographical location of his or her practice. Those who intend to practise as a barrister in a member state of the European Community must successfully complete the Vocational Course at the Inns of Court School of Law. Those who do not intend to practise as a barrister in a member state of the European Community, but who nevertheless wish to be called to the Bar of England and Wales, must successfully complete the Bar Examination and are not eligible (except in the limited circumstances described in the previous article) to enrol on the Vocational Course. Courses aimed at preparing candidates for the Bar Examination are no longer held at the Inns of Court School of Law, but are available at a number of other institutions.

Individuals who are already qualified as lawyers within the European Community but who have not been called to the Bar of England and Wales may seek to be called provided they obtain the approval of the Joint Regulations Committee of the Council of the Inns of Court and the General Council of the Bar, and that they pass appropriate sections of the aptitude test which is administered twice a year by the Inns of Court School of Law. The school does not run a course to prepare candidates for this test, but detailed information and reading lists are available from the school.

This article describes first the Vocational Course and then goes on to describe the format of the Bar Examination.

The Vocational Course

The emphasis of the course is on a practical training in the specialist skills required by barristers with the aim of ensuring competence in those skills which barristers use in practice. This is achieved through the practise of skills in the tasks most commonly performed by junior members of the Bar during the early years of practice. The majority of class contact time is devoted to learning skills. The novel nature of this programme of study has led the Council of Legal Education, in conjunction with Blackstone Press, to publish a series of manuals. These are provided for every student on the course, but they are also on general sale in legal bookshops.

Skills training

There are short introductory courses intended to develop an awareness of the importance of interpersonal skills and written skills for the barrister. These courses are completed during the first two weeks of the autumn term and form the foundation for the detailed teaching of the skills which have been identified as relevant to those practising at the Bar. These skills are: legal research, fact management, opinion writing, conference skills, negotiating, drafting and advocacy. These separate skills courses vary in length – some are very short, for example the course on conference skills takes only three hours, whilst others which involve a wide range of techniques are comparatively long, for example the drafting course consists of twenty-six hours of class contact time. Each of these barrister skills is taught initially in a separate course. Students are then encouraged to use the skills acquired in combination with one another in the realistic context of sets of papers of a kind and level of complexity which a junior barrister could be expected to receive during the very early years of practice. These practical training exercises form a major element of the course.

Teaching methods

Students learn skills by gaining experience of them in interactive classes and through dealing with realistic sets of case papers. Role play is thus a central part of the learning process. Students will interview one another, role playing the barrister, the lay and/or professional client, negotiate solutions to legal problems with one another as a barrister might, draft documents and pleadings as required, conduct cases in 'courts' and 'tribunals' both as barristers and as others in the trial process, carry out legal research using original source materials and practitioners' works, write opinions on the merits of a case, on quantum and on the evidence, and experience how to sort out a set of papers identifying facts available and those which are required, how they are to be proved and what inferences can be drawn; they will also practise developing and presenting a theory for the case and/or finding a solution to the problem presented.

The skills training is conducted in a very practical way. For most students, this will present a very different experience from that provided at the academic stage of training. In practice, following instructions and finding and sorting out facts and how to use them, are all of crucial importance, whereas the ability to write an academic essay on a point of law is of much less value. As students progress through the course and become competent in each skill, the papers presented will become more and more complex, requiring the use of all the skills outlined above in the way in which these would combine together in practice.

Legal knowledge in the context of skills training

The practical work will be based largely on the 'core legal subjects' studied as part of the academic stage of training. Sets of papers may include legal issues related to, for example, the law of contract or the law of tort. In addition, during the early part of the course, students will acquire a detailed knowledge of adjectival law (that is evidence, civil and criminal litigation), areas which will be of very great importance in carrying out the practical case work. In the third term, students will be given the opportunity to specialize in one of three fields of practice (namely, general practice, chancery practice or commercial practice) in which it is expected that the second six months' pupillage will be spent. In this part of the course the practical work concentrates on the kinds of task which a second six month pupil is likely to undertake in two areas of law which are a usual part of practice in the chosen field. Preparation for practice here is aimed at the second six months of pupillage, because this is the first opportunity which the pupil will have to practise independently on his/her feet, and such experience and understanding of the tasks likely to be encountered is a valuable mechanism for building up confidence and competence.

Preparation for pupillage
Finally, in the last weeks of the third term there is a short course to help prepare students for pupillage.

Legal knowledge on the Vocational Course

The overall aim is largely to build on the knowledge which has been acquired at the academic stage of training in such a way as to prepare students for practice rather than to extend knowledge purely for its own sake. The whole emphasis is therefore to encourage students to discover the knowledge which is needed to resolve a particular case for themselves and then to use that knowledge efficiently and effectively for that purpose. In simulating practice, students are encouraged to become used to the idea of being independent and in control of their own professional lives.

The legal knowledge required on the course can be divided into four areas:

That of which the barrister should have a detailed knowledge and understanding
The rules of evidence, civil litigation, criminal litigation, and the rules of professional conduct are crucial to a successful practice. Concentrated courses of study are provided in the earlier part of the course in these areas.

That of which every barrister should have a general understanding
Barristers need to be able to recognize all the consequences of particular courses of action: that is, all the remedies which could be appropriate in a particular case; sentencing practice and procedure; the potential and growing impact of European Community law; the basic structure and impact of the taxation system; an ability to read and understand basic accounts; and recognition of the legal ramifications of the different forms of business association. Short courses of study are provided for each of these areas.

That of which every barrister should have an overview
This knowledge is required because either it may influence the way in which a case is being conducted (so the potential impact of social security law, the European Convention on Human Rights, conflict of laws, the law of succession and legal aid is included), or because it is such a common field

of practice for the junior practitioner that some awareness of the legal area is necessary (that is, landlord and tenant law, family law and sale of goods and consumer credit law). Short courses of study or materials are provided for each of these areas.

That which the barrister should know about two specialist areas of law and procedure before embarking on the second six months of pupillage

These currently include: in the field of general practice, two specialist areas of law and procedure chosen from family law, employment law, sale of goods and consumer credit, landlord and tenant law and European Community law; in the field of chancery practice, two specialist areas of law and procedure chosen from trusts, tax and wills, conveyancing and real property, landlord and tenant law and company law; in the field of commercial practice, European Community law, the law of international trade, sale of goods and consumer credit and company law.

The assessment process

The whole thrust of the assessment process is to reduce the amount of rote learning which students have traditionally been required to do and to require students to commit to memory only such principles and rules as are deemed absolutely necessary for successful practice. Hence in adjectival law, where a detailed knowledge of legal principle and/or procedure is required, multiple choice tests are held to establish that students have acquired that knowledge to the requisite standard.

In so far as the assessment of skills is concerned the purpose is to establish whether a student has reached, at the very least, a competent standard in the skills which will be used in the second six months' pupillage and is capable of using legal principles and rules in a practical way. Assessments in skills are held both during the course (the in-course assessments) and at its end (the final assessment). In order to ensure that students recognize that the skills assessment process is intended to judge whether students can perform the skills which a barrister needs in practice and are not intended to test a student's memory of the law, students are allowed to use any materials provided for them during the course. Students are assessed on how they prepare for and carry out a number of tasks, so, for example, in an advocacy assessment, students will be judged on their competence as an advocate, not on their ability to remember and restate a number of theories of what makes a great advocate. Assessment criteria are specified for each assessment and so students will know what the assessors are looking for in the case.

The involvement of the Bar

Practising barristers play a considerable part in the teaching and assessing of skills on the Vocational Course and have given wholehearted support to the development of the new curriculum, the authorship of materials and the preparation of sets of case papers.

The Bar Examination

The Bar Examination continues in the same format as before for those who do not intend to practise as a barrister in any member state of the European Community and students may sit for the written examination at Trinity and Michaelmas in each year.

The examination consists of six papers: general paper I (involving the law of tort and criminal law), general paper II (involving the law of contract and equity and trusts), evidence, civil and criminal procedure and two optional papers chosen from the following: revenue law, family law (and procedure), sale of goods and credit, practical conveyancing, conflict of laws, the law of international trade, European Community law and human rights. In choosing which of these optional papers to take, students are not entitled to repeat subjects previously studied as part of a degree course.

The syllabus and recommended reading list for these papers are published each year in the Calendar. This can be purchased from the Inns of Court School of Law, as can examination papers from earlier years.

All the papers require a practical approach to be displayed, rather than an academic one. The papers require students to write opinions on the merits of the case and to give advice on matters of evidence and procedure and, where appropriate, sentence or quantum of damages, and to draft documents. Practise at these skills is crucial to success in the examination.

Pupillage and the practical training
DAVID LATHAM QC

David Latham is a QC practising in general common law in London. The former chairman of the Bar's working party on pupillage which reported in 1988, he is currently the Chairman of the Professional Standards Committee of the Bar Council.

Pupillage is the process by which the skills learnt in the vocational stage, and the law learnt at the academic stage are translated into practice. It is an exhilarating and painful experience. Exhilarating because there is no doubt that meeting real problems for the first time is rewarding, and the learning curve, however well the pupil has been prepared by both the academic and vocational stages, is steep. First appearances in court can be bruising. Not only is the pupil learning, but he or she is being constantly assessed to determine whether or not he or she is of barrister material, but also if he or she could be good enough to be taken on as a tenant in chambers at the end of pupillage.

The great strength of pupillage as a system is the relationship between the pupil and the pupil master. What may appear daunting in prospect is usually made not only acceptable but fun and enjoyable in practice by the support and help given by the pupil master. Whatever criticisms have been made about pupillage by those who have just been through it, the heartening message is that pupil masters have been conscientious and helpful.

The essence of pupillage is this close relationship between pupil master and pupil which enables the pupil to put the necessary skills into practice in three distinct stages: first by watching the way the pupil master works, this is by example; second by being able to practise the skills other than advocacy, such as pleading and advising, in circumstances where they can be monitored by the pupil master; third by being able to commence advocacy supported by the pupil master. Like any generalization, this does not reflect the course of every pupillage, particularly specialist pupillage, such as crime, where advocacy will be the overriding concern, or many chancery pupillages where the opportunity for advocacy may be infrequent. The great benefit of the system is that a very large proportion of learning process occurs more through a process of osmosis than by formal instruction.

Until 1988 there was little by way of control. The system had grown up and the Bar was small, and there was little if any need of formality. During the course of the overall review of training for the Bar it became apparent that the system should be improved, and the deficiences inherent in any relatively unstructured training system (however successful in practice) have been dealt with by some relatively simple, but significant, changes. Pupil masters, who have to be approved, are now registered on a central register and pupils, when commencing pupillage, register as pupils to a particular pupil master. At the end of the first six months, the pupil master is required to sign a certificate indicating that the pupil has completed six months' pupillage satisfactorily, in which event the pupil will in turn receive his or her practising certificate. Until such time as the Bar Council receives the pupil master's certificate, the pupil is not entitled to appear in court or accept instructions on his or her own behalf. At the end of the second six months, a similar process of certification occurs. The result is a full certificate for the pupil, who is thereafter entitled to practise entirely on his or her own account. Each chambers is required to provide the pupils with a check list of the basic syllabus which the chambers considers to be appropriate for the particular type of work in which it is engaged. The check list can either be what might be called a proforma check list provided by the Bar Council or through the specialist Bar Associations, or an individual check list for the particular set of chambers, which has been approved by the Bar Council. In this way, it is hoped that both pupil and pupil master can monitor the progress of pupillage, so as to ensure that all relevant topics have been covered; at the end of pupillage, the completed check list provides a record of the experience gained by each pupil.

During the course of this year, 1991/2, a pilot scheme for two hundred pupils is being run in order to evaluate a course of continuing education for pupils. It consists of four elements. First, a five-day course in accountancy and general business, and commercial structures and practices. Second, a two-day course in European and European Human Rights law. Third, a one-day course dealing with general problems relating to the practical side of running a practice, such as tax and VAT. Fourth, a two-day intensive advocacy course. By the time those reading this article have qualified, there will be yet further courses available to those who are in practice provided by circuits, specialist Bar Associations, and chambers themselves.

Payment to pupils? Ten years ago the Bar would have looked with surprise at anybody who had suggested such a thing. Apart from scholarships given by the Inns to the bright and the poor, pupillage was considered to be a privilege: indeed twenty years ago the pupil paid for that privilege. But in the last ten years things have changed dramatically. By five years ago, a significant number of chambers were providing modest awards out of their own funds. This has now progressed, not only under the stimulus of competition for the best graduate talent, but also within the Bar for the best students. The result is that most chambers now offering pupillage also offer financing support for some or all of their pupils. The amount of this support has been increased each year so that some commercial sets are now offering up to £20,000 for the pupillage year, and ordinary common law sets are seeking to provide that which the Bar Council recommends, which is at least £6,000 either by way of awards, or by way of guaranteed earnings, during the pupillage year. In some sets of chambers, the latter is an attractive option, because pupils can earn quite significant sums of money during their second six months of pupillage. Finance during the pupillage year should not be seen as a deterrent to those of the requisite ability who wish to come to the Bar.

While pupils are still expected to try and find their own pupillages, the new Bar Council computer programme called PATRIC is able to match those not fortunate enough to find their own places with the available vacancies. PATRIC also generates the contents of the Chambers, Pupillages and Awards Handbook which gives details of everything on offer, including mini-pupillages.

At the same time as seeking to improve the quality of pupillage for those wishing to practise in independent practice at the Bar, the Bar has significantly improved the process of training for those barristers who wish to enter employment as barristers. All now have to complete six months' pupillage in chambers but the second six months can be served with an employed pupil master. This has enabled the Crown Prosecution Service, the Government Legal Service, the armed forces, and private industry to put forward training programmes which have received the approval of the Bar Council, and which provide a great variety of opportunities. In many instances, these schemes involve payment to the pupil, not only for the period spent with the employed pupil master, but also for the period in chambers.

Part VI
The qualified career

The Criminal Bar

Members of the Criminal Bar spend most of their professional lives engaged in court work. The life of a typical junior will entail travelling from court to court appearing in a succession of cases. At the start of his/her career, the criminal practitioner will appear most frequently in the magistrates' courts, progressing to cases in the crown courts as he/she gains greater experience. Preparation for cases largely has to be done in the evenings, as the day is taken up by travelling, waiting and appearing in court. Occasionally, because instructions will have been received late in the day or returned by another member of the Bar, a case may have to be prepared in the evening for the hearing the next day. Most members of the Criminal Bar both prosecute and defend rather than specializing specifically in either prosecution or defence work.

Typically, most members of chambers are out at court during the day and return in the late afternoon for conferences, and to collect papers and briefs. This enables pupils both to hear how more experienced practitioners deal with situations in general and to join in discussion about the type of case which they may have dealt with for the first time that day.

The rates of pay and procedures for paying fees have improved enormously, which now results in pupils earning sums which should at least cover their living expenses towards the end of their pupillage. Pupils normally can expect to earn fees during the second six months' pupillage as pupils in criminal chambers frequently obtain cases in their own right during the period. Academic achievement is clearly welcomed at the Criminal Bar, but the hallmark of the criminal practitioner is common sense, robustness and a fluent court manner.

The criminal barrister exercises judgment on the evidence and the law in advising clients on their plea (if defending) or on whether or not to proceed (when prosecuting). When defending, any plea tendered must be the plea of a defendant freely entered although it is proper for the barrister to tender robust advice if the circumstances warrant it.

It is becoming common for senior members of the Criminal Bar, whether QCs or juniors, to sit as assistant recorders trying criminal cases.

The Family Law Bar

Family law work covers a wide spectrum of work involving disputes between individuals which arise in the context of their domestic relations, and disputes relating to children.

The largest area of work concerns property and financial provision following divorce, and disputes of all kinds in relation to children, whether between the two parents or between the parents and a local authority. Other work includes: provision for spouses and former spouses under the Inheritance Act 1985, where no provision has been made by the deceased spouse; divorce, judicial separation, nullity, recognition of foreign marriages; adoption. It involves also a knowledge of other complex areas of law including tax and private international law. Increasingly, cases are being taken to the European Court of Human Rights.

Family law work can be practised exclusively but is often combined with a general common law and/or criminal practice.

Non-litigious work involves the drafting of pleadings and affidavits and advisory work.

The work is rewarding because of the deep human problems which are encountered. However, it requires patience and special skills as the family practitioner has to act as counsellor and conciliator, as well as advocate.

The Chancery Bar

The Chancery Bar consists of those barristers who practise principally in the Chancery Division of the High Court. The work covers a wide variety of areas of practice whose common theme is 'property'. No two chancery practices are the same and emphases differ widely.

A general chancery practitioner may find himself doing any (or all) of the following: trusts; revenue – including especially inheritance tax; charities; company work; partnerships and other business arrangements (these may be of many sorts and most of them could well be described as 'commercial'); insolvency; land – including particularly the sale of land and interests in land such as rights of way and covenants; landlord and tenant including business tenancies and agricultural holdings; town and country planning (though rather less of this); probate, including contested probate of wills, family provision and the administration of estates; court of protection; mortgages and other commercial securities; many commercial matters with a property/money/banking element.

There are some tighter degrees of specialization; thus, there are chambers who do predominantly company and insolvency work and others which specialize in landlord and tenant work. There are pure revenue specialists and patents specialists. Most chancery chambers have particular 'house' specializations.

The chancery practitioners appear in court far more than they once did, although the amount of time which any individual practitioner spends in court will vary.

The majority of chancery sets are in London but it is perfectly possible to be a chancery practitioner in the larger provincial areas.

The work undertaken by the Chancery Bar is of a demanding nature, requiring academic aptitude and the ability to express oneself clearly in writing as well as orally. Each set has its own entry requirements but, as a general guide, no serious entrant ought to have less than a good honours degree, ie at least upper second.

The prospects for success are good, both in terms of monetary reward and job satisfaction. As a general indication, whilst beginners in their first year cannot expect to make much profit, after ten years' earnings of between £40,000 and £50,000 net per annum can be expected.

The Revenue Bar

Revenue work is substantially advisory and comprises such areas of work as how to minimize the taxation of proposed transactions and the taxation consequences of transactions which have already taken place.

Practitioners therefore work in some or all of: income tax, corporation tax, capital gains tax, value added tax, inheritance tax, stamp duty and petroleum revenue tax.

A significant element of work involves the resolution of liabilities where there has been under-declaration in the past.

Practitioners, for the most part, do not often become involved in a great deal of litigation in court. They do, however, appear from time to time before the General Commissioners and the Special Commissioners of the Inland Revenue.

The Revenue Bar Association has approximately ninety members of whom about fifty practise in all or most of the areas mentioned above; the remainder practise in a specific area in conjunction with the use of their expertise in another field, for example a specialist in inheritance tax might also specialize in chancery work.

The London Common Law and Commercial Bar Association

The London Common Law and Commercial Bar Association represents the interests of London-based barristers practising in civil law. Members' practices encompass such widely diverse fields as international trade, personal injuries, revenue, planning, landlord and tenant and environmental law.

The demands of the marketplace, the considerable increase in areas of substantive law and the impact of Europe have resulted in today's London common and commercial lawyers developing specialist areas of practice. The focus of many members' work is litigation in the Queen's Bench Division or for more junior barristers in the county courts. Such work includes sale of goods, product liability, banking, professional negligence, administrative or construction law. As the name of the Association implies many of its members practise wholly or mainly at the Commercial Bar and are involved, for example, in international trade, shipping or insurance matters.

In the 1990s, disputes involving what might be termed general 'business law' may equally be heard by a commercial court judge, a Chancery judge or a Queen's Bench judge. This flexibility highlights the true skill or specialization of the London common or commercial lawyer: as an advocate in the conduct of litigation. But although the majority of the work of the members of the Association concerns litigation in one way or another – whether it be an appearance at a trial or a pre-trial hearing, the drafting of pleadings or the giving of advice – a more general advisory service is also provided, for example, the drafting of terms of business agreements or other non-litigious documents.

The work of members also includes appearances in arbitrations and before a wide variety of standing and *ad hoc* tribunals and inquiries.

The Association is regularly invited to provide its views upon proposed changes in the law, both substantive and procedural, emanating both nationally and from Europe.

The Association piloted and now administers an arbitration scheme known as the London Bar Arbitration Scheme.

The Commercial Bar Association (COMBAR)

The Commercial Bar Association (COMBAR) is composed of commercial chambers and individual practitioners at the Commercial Bar.

The Commercial Bar primarily services the specialist legal needs of the City of London, particularly international commercial litigation and arbitration. It gives advice to clients from all over the world, reflecting the importance of London as an international commercial and financial centre and as a forum for the resolution of international disputes.

Its principal fields of practice are: international trade, shipping and aviation, banking and financial services, insurance and reinsurance, commodity transactions, insolvency, mergers and acquisitions, competition law, intellectual property, professional negligence, licensing, judicial review of governmental acts, employment, European Community matters and public international law.

Some of the particular services offered by members of COMBAR are:

(a) acceptance of direct instructions from overseas lawyers and other professional advisers
(b) advice on legal matters and disputes and other matters arising anywhere in the world
(c) acting as advocates in overseas courts and tribunals of the European Community, Singapore, Hong Kong, Malaysia, Caribbean Islands, Bermuda and elsewhere
(d) acting as advocates in international arbitrations in England or elsewhere – more international and commercial arbitration takes place in London than in any other city in the world
(e) giving evidence as an expert on English law in courts or arbitrations elsewhere in the world.

The Patent Bar

Practitioners at the Patent Bar do not deal with patent matters alone. They are generally specialists in all kinds of intellectual property law including the law of patents, registered designs, copyright, trademarks and passing off. Many practitioners also specialize in the law of breach of confidence, which has much in common with more orthodox intellectual property.

The work inevitably requires the practitioner to grasp matters of technical and scientific complexity which require an aptitude for scientific problems. The vast majority of practitioners in this field therefore have some form of scientific qualification, and/or scientific experience. Such qualifications may well be a significant factor in the recruitment of pupils.

By the very nature of intellectual property, much litigation involves applications for interlocutory injunctions in the High Court, such work often being done by junior barristers. A great deal of time is also taken up with paperwork for, as a specialist adviser, a practitioner will be heavily involved in the preparation for such applications. As practitioners become more senior, they will do less interlocutory work, and take on more full actions, which can be extremely complex and lengthy.

In addition to High Court work, the patent practitioner also appears at hearings in the Patent Office and the Trade Marks Registry.

On the non-litigious side, advice may be sought on potential patent, trademark and copyright infringements, the question of validity of patents and trademarks and the drafting of licensing agreements. Questions of European law may well arise in this context and practitioners should have at least a working knowledge of the competition provisions of the Treaty of Rome.

Patent practitioners are increasingly being asked to advise in highly technical contractual disputes, particularly those involving computer technology.

Patent practitioners are entitled to take instructions directly from patent and trademark agents as well as from solicitors.

The Administrative Law Bar

Members of the Bar practising in administrative law are concerned with applications for judicial review in the High Court and appearances before tribunals and inquiries. The subject matter of judicial review is the development of the body of general principles which govern the exercise of powers and duties by public authorities and inferior tribunals in many fields.

Local government, immigration (including habeas corpus and extradition), housing, homeless persons, town and country planning, education, social security, employment and licensing are all topics which figure prominently in the case law on the subject. Recently there have been a number of applications by companies in commercial and tax areas. In the last few years there have been important judicial review decisions involving local authorities in the spheres of rating and budgetary policy. Applications for judicial review can be made in both civil and criminal matters.

Examples of public bodies that have been challenged include government departments such as DHSS, the Home Office, the Ministry of Defence and the Law, and local government activities such as area and district health, local housing and police authorities. The courts and tribunals involved include the High Court, the Immigration Appeal Tribunal, the Parole Board and Prison Governors. Domestic and professional bodies include the Professional Conduct Committees of the Law Society and the Bar, Public corporations and other regulatory bodies include the BBC and London Regional Transport. Applications have also been made against educational institutions including universities and school governors.

Town and country planning and supplementary benefits are the two main areas of the law relating to public administration which involve preparation for and attendance at tribunals and inquiries. Types of tribunals include rent tribunals, local valuation courts (rating), mental health review tribunals and family practitioners committees.

The Local Government and Planning Bar

The work of the Local Government and Planning Bar principally concerns disputes with or relating to public authorities, which are mainly but not exclusively local authorities. Most, but not all, of these disputes relate in some way to land. The areas most commonly covered include town and country planning, compulsory purchase, highways, rating, housing and the general administration of local government. There is a significant amount of advisory work.

As far as the advocacy side of the work is concerned, much of it is undertaken at public inquiries, of which planning inquiries are the most common type. Appearances are also required in courts at all levels including the High Court and the Lands Tribunal.

There are not a great number of specialist practitioners in this field, probably in the region of 120 regulars. This roughly corresponds with the number of the Local Government and Planning Bar. Most are members of specialist sets of chambers in London which deal with this type of work. There are a number of individuals who have expert knowledge in this area but also practise in general common law or other areas.

Some of the work falls squarely into the wider field of 'administrative law'. There is also an overlap in the sense that some practitioners at the Local Government and Planning Bar regularly do other work in more or less related fields. An interesting example perhaps is that most of the members of the Parliamentary Bar, whose work includes the promotion of or opposition to private and local bills before parliamentary committees, are also practitioners at the Local Government and Planning Bar.

Official referees and the Bar

The construction industry (taking building and engineering together) is by most criteria the largest single industrial activity in the United Kingdom economy, and is extensively employed abroad. It is served by the large and well-organized professions of architects, engineers and surveyors, and by specialist solicitors and barristers.

Construction contracts are complicated and disputes are frequent. Many of these disputes are resolved by arbitrators, but an ever-increasing number are tried by official referees. There are up to ten official referees' courts, which are part of the High Court, sitting at the Royal Courts of Justice.

The official referees have their unusual title because they used to have cases 'referred' to them by judges of the High Court, perhaps for a report on matters of detail such as accountancy or surveying evidence. Nowadays they are specialist judges in their own right and try almost all the construction cases in the High Court.

There are perhaps sixty or seventy barristers who confine their work almost entirely to construction cases (the Construction Bar), and a considerably larger number of members of the Bar who appear in such cases fairly frequently and could be said to be specialists. The Construction Bar as such is largely concentrated in two sets of chambers.

Work at the 'Construction Bar' is arduous by reason of the size and complexity of the cases and much of the work is done before arbitrators. There is overseas work, particularly for QCs. The rewards can be great. Official referees are generally appointed from QCs who have already achieved distinction in other fields.

Members of the Construction Bar frequently have professional qualifications as surveyors or engineers. Potential practitioners in this field should consider carefully whether to commence their career elsewhere; for example in industry, or as barristers practising in common law chambers.

Barristers in commerce, finance and industry

DAVID FLETCHER ROGERS

David Fletcher Rogers is a Barrister and was the proposer and joint founder of the Bar Association for Commerce, Finance and Industry. His career has largely been as a member of a legal department of one of the great British companies with subsidiaries worldwide.

For many years barristers have been employed as in-house counsel who are recognized as valuable members of the business management team.

What barristers in business do

Naturally, one of the main ways in which barristers (both men and women) employed in business use their knowledge of the law is as staff legal advisers to companies or other organizations. In one way or another the law affects every part of a company's activities – from finance and mergers to the protection of patents and trademarks and international trade. With increasing legislation particularly with regard to environmental matters and EC law, management relies more and more on the advice and services of the trained in-house lawyer.

Increasingly, barristers are rising to the most senior managerial appointments in industry and a legal qualification offers an excellent avenue to a directorship to those lawyers who are prepared to broaden the horizons of their knowledge and acquire a thorough grasp of business techniques and methods. Lawyers occupy posts such as chairman, managing director, director and company secretary in commercial, financial and industrial organizations and thus their career structure is not confined solely to membership of legal departments.

So the job of the barrister employed in business is both important and full of interest. Whenever new developments in the company are being planned his/her contribution will be sought at an early stage. In the course of one week a barrister might be found advising on a new form of contract, participating at a conference to discuss expansion plans and travelling overseas to advise a foreign subsidiary company or to negotiate a contract with a customer. Even at the beginning of their business career they will usually enjoy an overall view of the company's operations and may well be asked to advise at board level, helping to influence decisions rather than merely executing them.

Your choice of career

If you decide to become a lawyer, you have two choices before you. You can become a barrister or a solicitor; and in either case you can go into private practice, or you can choose to make your career in business, the civil service or local government.

In making these choices, you may find it useful to bear in mind the following factors among others. To make a successful legal career in commerce, finance or industry you need to develop three qualities in particular:

(i) Clarity of thought, with the ability to 'see both the wood and the trees' in a complex situation, and to find a practical solution to any legal problem which is disclosed as a result. The process of studying law itself helps to develop this quality.
(ii) A good commercial sense, so that you can advise on the best course of action within the law to achieve the business objectives in view.
(iii) In many jobs, the ability to negotiate business deals as well as to advise on their legal implications.

The work done by barristers and solicitors in employment is very similar and many employers do not distinguish between the two branches of the profession when recruiting for legal appointments. BACFI has, with some success, promoted the view that employed barristers should enjoy, as a minimum, equal professional rights and standing with employed solicitors. The current reviews being undertaken by the Lord Chancellor's Advisory Committee will amend the Code of Conduct to the extent necessary to remove historic limitations that cannot be justified in the modern practice.

The great tradition of the Bar of England and Wales, and membership of an Inn of Court – carrying with it the opportunity of meeting and conversing with experienced members over lunch or dinner in the Hall of the Inn – have an attraction for many prospective lawyers.

Pupillage

A barrister is not allowed to practise alone at the Bar until he or she has served as a pupil of a practising barrister for at least twelve months, although it is possible to appear in court and earn fees himself during the second six months of pupillage.

A barrister taking a position in business need not have served a pupillage although most employers consider the experience gained as a pupil to be an advantage; indeed from a barrister's own point of view it is desirable that he/she undergoes pupillage. A pupil must spend the first six months of pupillage in chambers but can choose to spend the second six with an employed pupil master.

Commercial pupils

Some legal departments offer a scheme whereby barristers are taken on as pupils in order to give them business-oriented training, but these opportunities are comparatively few and eagerly sought.

The Bar Association for Commerce, Finance and Industry (BACFI)

This was founded in 1965 and is the professional Association for barristers employed in business. It is very active in enhancing the position of the employed barristers and BACFI has representatives on the Bar Council and its committees, Benchers of the Inns of Court and other legal bodies. BACFI is also an active member of ECLA – the European Company Lawyers Association.

One of its functions is to provide occasions for barristers to meet together to review problems and opportunities in the business world.

At present there is a great demand for competent lawyers in industry with the ever increasing amount of new law in the form of Acts of Parliament EC Directives, regulations and codes of practice.

To find out about using BACFI one should write to The Secretary, BACFI, 2 Plowden Buildings, Middle Temple Lane, London EC4Y 9AT.

What jobs are available to the newly qualified?

It may be a little difficult to get a job straight from pupillage as employers tend to look for experienced lawyers.

This is where BACFI can be helpful: with its record of those companies which may take recently qualified people as well as those who have had a commercial pupillage.

There is always an opportunity for qualified lawyers to show ability and initiative.

Anyone thinking of going into business as a lawyer should write to some of the companies with large legal departments to see what vacancies exist doing almost anything.

Companies like people to show initiative, and many companies take on students or newly qualified lawyers during the summer months. The work will be rather routine but it will give you, and the legal department, an opportunity of judging whether you are suited to working in commercial surroundings.

What are the qualities for a successful lawyer in industry?

- He or she must have ability coupled with common sense – the ability to distinguish between worthwhile points and others.
- It is essential to have the type of personality whereby you get on with people at all levels.
- People must learn to have confidence in you; this means if a mistake is made you admit it and do not try and cover it up.
- You must be master of your subject area. In business there are a wide range of legal topics, some needing their own special knowledge and skills such as industrial relations, copyright, patents, commercial contracts, turnkey projects, health and safety at work, competition law, including EC, licensing trademarks, company law and many others, including some as interesting as anti-counterfeiting work.

The successful lawyer will be a specialist in certain areas, and must be able to recognize when a problem arises outside his/her speciality in order to refer it to a colleague or for external specialist advice.

The contrast between private practice and in-house

The most important difference is that in-house lawyers generally do creative legal work – it can be the formation of profitable companies, the licensing of inventions for royalty or the setting up of joint ventures – projects which will lead to employment opportunities.

Contrast the position of the barrister in private practice who, by and large, does remedial legal work, such as seeking damages for injury, husbands/wives desperate for divorce, remedies being sought for broken contracts and criminals to be jailed. All these events occur as a result of something going wrong.

It is more satisfying for many to know that their contributions in practising law are constructive.

On the inside looking out

The in-house counsel knows at an early stage what is happening and is part of a project team from beginning to end. They may travel extensively, which for the younger person has attractions, and will become conversant in many cases with overseas law and developments. They must be forward-looking and proactive rather than reactive, that is, guide their employers to prevent trouble arising rather than dealing with the consequence of the employers going wrong – though of course this does occur.

The in-house person also knows his/her employer's business thoroughly, which makes legal work so much more interesting.

Such is the complexity of present-day law that the in-house lawyer in all but the largest companies will need to be in touch with private practitioners for specialized advice, and over the years one builds up relationships with solicitors and with members of the Independent Bar. It is, more and more, an important function of the in-house lawyer to see that external advisers are fully and adequately instructed and that their work is correctly monitored.

The quality of the work and its rewards

It is very worthwhile and the rewards are good. The senior legal adviser of a large company will command a salary in the region of £70,000 with a car, plus in many cases bonuses and share options which are becoming increasingly popular and indeed can, and do, make people quite rich. At the start, one's first job will be paid about £18,000–£20,000 according to location. Promotion up the salary scale is swift because if a company has good lawyers they know they must pay to keep them.

Once a lawyer has had two to three years' commercial experience there should be no difficulty in moving to another post as many do in their early years to gain experience.

There is now no discrimination against women, who have more and more opportunities to get to the top – Kodak Ltd, for example, have recently appointed a woman to be company secretary as well as head of the legal division.

Transferring from the Bar to the Law Society

Under the Qualified Lawyers Transfer Regulations 1990, a barrister wishing to qualify as a solicitor is required either to have served twelve months in pupillage and twelve months in legal practice acceptable to the Law Society, or two years in legal practice acceptable to the Law Society, or such period not exceeding two years as the Society may determine in a solicitor's office, employed in a way compatible with articles and pass the Professional Conduct and Accounts paper set in the Qualified Lawyers Transfer Test.

Eacy year some five hundred barristers transfer to become solicitors and this number is steadily rising.

Part VII
The directory

How to select a firm of solicitors

Articles of this type usually divide into two groups. There are those which give logical instructions leading to a conclusion about which there is little argument, and there are others which are not so clear cut and require subjective judgments. Unfortunately this article falls squarely into the latter category.

There are thousands of solicitors' firms in this country from which to choose and probably the best approach is to consider a list of questions. This enables you to establish the criteria for an acceptable firm and so narrow down the choice. The questions vary depending on which you are: a businessman who wants to retain a firm, a student who wishes to train with one, or a qualified solicitor changing firms or moving back into practice.

The businessman

To the businessman the Law Society, operating through its local branches, is able to offer a great deal of guidance and advice. This support can perhaps be complemented by a list of questions:

(a) Where must the firm have offices? How far away can your main contact office be from your premises, and do you have other plants, sites or branches around the country which need offices near them?

(b) Do you need a firm with a large international office network or with representation in a particular continent or country, or is your business really only in the UK?

(c) Does your business have any especially complicated or obscure aspects which might require the firm retained to have a particular skill or expertise?

(d) Do you want to retain a firm as general legal advisers, or do you also wish it to possess specialist departments?

(e) Will the character or size of your business change in the near future? If so, what extra requirements will arise?

(f) What type of firm do your competitors use and why?

(g) What type of firm do your other advisers (eg banker, auditor) recommend?

(h) Do you have any personal experience of, or connection with, any firms?

Having used this list to obtain a manageable number of practices, it is then quite acceptable to visit each in turn and discuss your needs with a partner. This enables you to gain a first impression and the discussions are always useful. More than one may have to exclude itself from consideration for a range of possible ethical and practical reasons, and partners are also quite open if they feel you would be more suited to another firm. Their aim is to build a long-term relationship – a brief and uncomfortable one serves nobody's interests. Ultimately, however, the choice must be the firm with which you feel most at ease. You will have to share much confidential information and rely on the partner's advice, and therefore trust and a common viewpoint are essential for both parties.

The potential trainee solicitor

The student or school-leaver reading this part of the guide is in a rather different position. 'Articles', the period when you add practical training and experience to the theory you have learnt, are available in many different places – in local government, industry and commerce, magistrates' courts and a few law centres. However, because the majority take articles in private practice, this section is addressed at them, though little changes for those considering other paths of admission to the Roll of Solicitors. You have three main requirements. You want a good training leading as painlessly as possible to qualification, a wide variety of work experience to ensure a good development of your professional skills, and finally, an interesting working life in a pleasant environment.

The first requirement is very seldom a problem as the Law Society keeps a close watch on the calibre of training offered by firms to their trainee solicitors and the firms themselves have every incentive to support you. The second two are more subjective in that different people prefer different types of practice. Once again, a list of questions may help to crystallize your thoughts and narrow the choice.

(a) Where do you wish to train? Do you want the office to be near your home, school, university or polytechnic, or do you wish to live and work somewhere new?
(b) What size of firm do you want to work for? Large firms say they offer a comprehensive array of national and international resources and opportunities. Medium sized ones claim to give the trainee solicitor

all that he or she can benefit from, usually with a range of national and international links, while still not losing the personal touch. Small firms consider that they alone offer a personal and almost continuous training, with far greater client involvement and daily contact with the partners.

(c) What kind of training package do you want? Various types are available, with each firm offering different mixes and amounts of in-house classes and seminars on professional and managerial skills.

(d) What type of client work interests you? While solicitors will turn their hands to most things at the request of clients, it is still true that certain firms consider themselves specialists in particular types of business. Such specialization may be more evident at an office level. Thus, a firm's Central London office is likely to have more service sector clients and fewer manufacturers than an office of the same firm in the Midlands, and a large City practice is likely to place heavy emphasis on company commercial work. There is a similar choice to be made about the size of client you would prefer. Large organizations tend to retain similar sized firms. If you join a partnership with a portfolio of such clients, you will inevitably deal with their problems. However, a smaller firm could say – with some fairness – that you seldom see the full picture and become a cog in the machine, and may not work with the same people again. They would instead offer earlier responsibility and greater work continuity, though with fewer of your clients making the front page of *The Times*.

(e) When do you wish to join a firm? Not all can be flexible.

(f) What is a firm's overtime policy for trainee solicitors?

(g) Do you want to join a specialist department? Some firms offer the option of training in specialist departments from the start.

(h) Looking ahead to the day you qualify, what do you think you would then like to do? It would obviously be best if you chose initially to stay in practice to be able to continue your career without having to change firms.

As for the businessman, this list of questions should enable you to reduce your choice to a few firms which can then be approached. Many offer open days and other informal contacts before you decide to make a formal application.

The qualified solicitor

Such a person may feel they need less guidance as to which firm to select. However, if only for completeness, set out below are a few thoughts which may help to make the choice clearer.

(a) Are you keen to work in a general practice or do you want to be a specialist and if so, of what kind? Some firms may not have the department of your choice or only a small one.
(b) Does your work experience have any glaring omissions you wish to fill, or does any aspect of it make you particularly attractive to a firm?
(c) What kind of salary package do you want, bearing in mind the cost of living in an area and its general desirability?
(d) What are the prospects for promotion and what level of responsibility are you looking for?
(e) Do you want the option of an overseas secondment or one to a client?
(f) What is a firm's attitude to staff who wish to change departments? Is it easy to move across to a different specialist unit or to go to a different office?
(g) What are your long-term aims, and how will your choice of firm affect their attainment?

Finally, as a member of the Law Society, you can always discuss your position with them. While they obviously cannot recommend a particular firm, the staff are very helpful in other ways, as are the local law societies, for which contact details are given in the first part of the guide.

Using the directory

The following pages contain a directory representing a cross-section of UK solicitors' firms, each of which has provided a comprehensive profile. A complete list of members and firms is published annually under the direction of the Law Society, and details of particular ones can be obtained from the local law societies.

The information given in the profiles is an amalgam of that most frequently requested by students, businessmen and members of the profession. Firms write their own entries, using a proforma, to ensure their accuracy. The information they supply is thus directly comparable. The only variations are a minor rewording of the line headings where this gives a more accurate picture (for example, some firms have senior rather than managing partners), and the omission of irrelevant lines (such as where a firm has no overseas offices). However, care must be taken when interpreting trainee solicitor salary figures. Predictions two years hence are of limited value, so many firms have indicated what they currently offer or looked forward only as far as 1993.

The directory has been arranged in alphabetical order, and the writers were encouraged to try and convey the maximum possible factual information in the space available. This year eighteen entries were submitted for inclusion and it is hoped to continue this growth in future editions, thereby adding to the usefulness of this part of the guide.

The Law Society Careers & Recruitment Service

The Law Society Careers & Recruitment Service is a free and confidential service to appliants, and experienced consultants will be happy to give you advice on any aspect of your career.

Qualified solicitors
Applicants seeking a move within the profession are invited to submit a comprehensive curriculum vitae or fill out a registration form (available from the office), returning it by post to a consultant at the address opposite.

You will then be contacted either by telephone, if permissible (discretion assured), or by letter to discuss your requirements in depth. If practical, we will also be happy to arrange a confidential chat at our offices. Based on our understanding of your requirements, your details will be forwarded to a selection of appropriate vacancies currently on our files, and we will then contact you when we have generated positive interest from a client. We will of course be happy to discuss specific vacancies before submitting your details, if this is preferred.

Trainee and newly qualified solicitors
The Law Society Careers & Recruitment Service publishes a free monthly list of vacancies for *Immediately Available* trainee solicitors, ie those who have completed, or who are about to complete their Law Society Finals. Telephone: 071-320 5940 for further details.

The Law Society Careers & Recruitment Service publishes a free monthly list of vacancies for those who have been qualified for eighteen months or less who are looking for a position. Telephone 071-320 5940 for further details.

Equal opportunity policy
The Law Society Careers & Recruitment Service is committed to a policy of equal opportunities for all applicants irrespective of sex, race and disability.

Should you wish to discuss any aspects of the Service further, or to place a current vacancy, please contact the Manager, Jenny Goddard.

THE LAW SOCIETY
CAREERS & RECRUITMENT SERVICE

The official Recruitment Service of the Law Society

227/228 The Strand
London
WC2R 1BA

Telephone 071-242 1222
DX56 Chancery Lane

THE LAW SOCIETY'S CAREERS & RECRUITMENT SERVICE is a response to the obvious need within the profession for a recruitment service which offers candidates career guidance and choice through the contacts and resources of the Law Society and offers firms the best aspects of the commercial agencies at a more reasonable price. The service is confidential to both firms and applicants.

Allen & Overy

Main office: 9 Cheapside, London EC2V 6AD. Tel: 071-248 9898; Fax: 071-236 2192.
Overseas offices: Brussels, Dubai, Hong Kong, Madrid, New York, Paris, Tokyo, Warsaw.
Senior Partner: J M Kennedy.
Number of partners: 108 worldwide as at January 1992.
Number of professional staff: Over 550 worldwide.
Number of other staff: Over 500 worldwide.
Firm history: Founded in 1930, Allen & Overy is one of the largest firms in the country. With its main office in the City of London and a network of offices in all the world's financial centres, the practice has always concentrated on commercial work with a substantial international element.
Firm structure: While the practice is run on an efficient partnership model, more important to our success is the style of the firm. We enjoy our work and our aim is to serve our clients in the most progressive and effective way possible, whether this be through specifically tailored teams drawn from our pool of experts or the individual attention of a partner or other solicitor.
Major events in the past year: Important developments during 1991 included the opening of our office in Warsaw further emphasizing Allen & Overy's commitment to an international practice.
Range of client services: The main areas of the firm's work are company and commercial (including international and domestic banking, insolvency, corporate finance and bonds), litigation, property, private client, EC and competition law and corporate taxation, with other specialist areas covering pensions, share incentives, employment, intellectual property and construction.
Number of trainee solicitors required for 1994: Approximately 65.
Minimum academic requirements: Applications are welcomed from both law and non-law graduates. At least an upper second class degree standard is expected.
Starting salary: £17,250 per annum in September 1991.
Number of qualified solicitors required for 1992: We are always interested in applications from first-class qualified solicitors.
Starting salary: £26,500 per annum in September 1991.
Annual leave entitlement: 22 days plus bank holidays.
Professional development policies and programmes: We offer a first-class, structured training programme which continues after articles, assistant solicitors are recruited primarily from our trainees, seventy-six of the present partners were articled with the firm.
For brochure and application form contact: Gideon Hudson.

HELP FOR THE GRADUATE WHO IS WONDERING WHICH WAY TO TURN

Choosing between law firms can be bewildering. Many firms offer benefits which, on paper, are not very different. However, the substance behind the words may vary a great deal.

Three features of Allen & Overy taken together make the firm very special to those that work here.

First, the quality of work handled by the firm and its professionalism. Qualifying with Allen & Overy is widely and properly regarded as a sign of quality.

Second, the emphasis placed on training at Allen & Overy is second to none. We want to help you achieve your full potential for your sake, and ours!

Third, the quality most often remarked on about Allen & Overy is the atmosphere; informal and friendly but busy and efficient. The key is the people we recruit.

If you would like to know more please contact: Gideon Hudson.

ALLEN & OVERY

9 CHEAPSIDE, LONDON EC2V 6AD

TELEPHONE: 071-248 9898   FACSIMILE: 071-236 2192

BRUSSELS · DUBAI · HONG KONG · MADRID · NEW YORK · PARIS · TOKYO · WARSAW

Ashurst Morris Crisp

Main office: Broadwalk House, 5 Appold Street, London EC2A 2HA.
Tel: 071-638 1111; Fax: 071-972 7990; Telex: 887067.
Overseas offices: Ashursts has offices in Brussels, Paris and Tokyo. The firm is also the UK member of Le Club, an international association of major corporate law firms in Europe and the United States.
Senior Partner: M G H Bell.
Number of partners: 50 plus 34 senior associates.
Number of other professional staff: 132
Number of other staff: 259
Firm history: Ashursts was founded in 1821 and has ranked among the leading City law firms throughout its history. Stock Exchange related transactions provide the single most important area of the firm's work and Ashursts is currently fourth among English law firms for the number of Stock Market clients.
Firm structure: The practice comprises five departments, these are: company and commercial; property and planning; litigation; tax and banking.
Range of client services: Ashurst Morris Crisp draws nearly all its clients from the business sector. It provides a full range of services for corporate clients: acquisitions, disposals, corporate finance, banking, management buy-outs, tax, pensions, commercial property and litigation advice.

The firm's fundamental aim is to provide practical advice which resolves a client's problems.
Number of trainee solicitors required for 1994: 25 (**recruited for 1993**: 25).
Minimum academic requirements: The firm concentrates on recruiting people who have excellent academic ability and who it believes will be able to communicate and work easily with colleagues and clients. Both law and non-law graduates who have broad interests, a practical outlook and a sense of humour are encouraged to apply.
Starting salary: £17,000 (1991) – under review.
Annual leave entitlement: 20 days.
Professional development policies and programmes: During articles a trainee solicitor undertakes practical training in those areas of law in which the firm practises. A trainee solicitor will spend time within three of the five main departments, normally directly supervised by a partner. Each will experience a broad range of work in the department in which he or she sits during articles. The firm places great emphasis upon training and has an extensive programme including regular seminars, know-how groups and skills training sessions for trainee solicitors and qualified solicitors.
Brochure available from: Edward Sparrow to whom applications should be made with a curriculum vitae.

Ashursts' places great importance on the careful selection of articled clerks, with the object of training them to be top-class City solicitors. It sees this as a key factor in the future strength and success of the firm.

The firm's philosophy is to give articled clerks as much responsibility as they can individually manage. Throughout they are treated as part of "the team" and are expected to play an intelligent and active role in each matter they become involved in.

"No articled clerk will reach the end of articles without having created an impression and having established a reputation within the firm."

However, it's not all work; the quality and frequency of Ashursts' social events are well known. Apart from a biennial dinner dance for all members of the firm and their respective partners (last held at the Savoy) Ashursts hosts an informal Christmas party for the whole firm. There are regular parties organised by members of staff and frequent social gatherings following lectures and sports events.

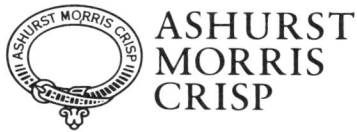

Broadwalk House, 5 Appold Street, London EC2A 2HA Telephone 071-638 1111
Telex 887067 Facsimile 071-972 7990 CDE Box number 639

CONTACT FORM

To: The Head of Recruitment

....

....

....

THE IVANHOE GUIDE TO
THE LEGAL PROFESSION 1992

I have been interested to read about your organization in the above publication and would be grateful if you would send me a copy of your brochure and an application form.

Signed.. Date..

*Name ....

*Address..

....

*Please print

Beachcroft Stanleys

Main office: 20 Furnival Street, London EC4A 1BN. Tel: 071-242 1011; Fax: 071-430 1532; Telex: 264607 (BEALAW G): DX 45 London.
Senior Partner: Andrew D Kennedy.
Number of partners: 32
Total fee earners: 120
Number of staff: 250
Firm history: The firm's origins extend back to 1762 in London with strong historical connections also with Bristol and Liverpool. The firm in its present form dates from 1988 with the amalgamation of Beachcrofts and Stanleys & Simpson North.
Firm structure: The firm is organized into four departments representing the major divisions of work undertaken: business, litigation, private client and property. A partner ensures the properly coordinated use of the firm's specialist services to meet the needs of a client. The business of the firm is run by a professional management team which leaves partners with their hands free to make the most active contribution to clients.
Range of client services: Beachcroft Stanleys is a medium sized City of London practice providing comprehensive legal service for a wide range of clients both from the United Kingdom and, increasingly, from overseas. Our clients extend from the family company to the publicly listed company; from the world of advertising to the world of accountants and surveyors; from banks and insurance companies to charitable institutions; from computer technology to property development and management; from water companies to health authorities and educational bodies. The firm also has many private clients, many of whose interests are connected with the firm's commercial practice.
Number of trainee solicitors required for 1994: 10
Starting salary: £15,500 (September 1991).
Minimum academic requirements: At least a good second class honours degree (we are happy to consider non-law graduates) but we also place much store on a wider record of activity and experience.
Professional development policies and programmes: A trainee solicitor's programme of training involves spending time in at least three of the departments but, where practicable, with experience in all four. Progress through articles of training is monitored on an individual basis by the firm's Director of Training and a programme of personal development is mapped out for each trainee solicitor. This programme continues where the trainee solicitor continues as an assistant solicitor with the firm. Internal courses and seminar programmes are arranged and, where appropriate, attendance at outside conferences is provided for.
For brochure and application form contact: Dafydd Evans (Director of Training).

Berwin Leighton

Main office: Adelaide House, London Bridge, London EC4R 9HA. Tel: 071-623 3144; Fax: 071-623 4416; Telex: 886420.
Other offices: 135 East 57th Street, New York NY10022. Tel: (0101 212) 754 5400; Fax: (0101 212) 754 5401. The firm has created an extensive network of links with firms both in the EC and internationally.
Chairman: Malcolm Brummer.
Principal Executive: Oonagh Harpur.
Number of partners: 51
Number of staff: 403 (including partners)
Firm history and structure: Berwin Leighton was formed in 1970 as a result of the merger of two smaller firms. Since then it has grown rapidly and is now a well respected medium sized City firm. It has recently undergone considerable managerial reorganization both at fee-earner level in the setting up of a formal departmental structure and at the business management level through the creation of a Board and the appointment of a comprehensive management support team.
Range of client services: We offer the full complement of legal, technical and commercial advice required by a wide range of corporate clients. We are market leaders in the field of property development with a special reputation in planning, the environment and secured lending. Increasingly we are acknowledged for our work in civil litigation, banking and European Community commercial law. We also provide expert advice in the areas of corporate and asset finance, insurance and reinsurance, shipping and aviation.
Number of trainees required for 1994: 15
Minimum academic requirements: 2.2. Non-law graduates considered.
Starting salary: £16,750 (September 1991).
Annual leave entitlement: 22 days.
Professional development policies and programmes: Trainees spend at least six months in each of the three major departments – corporate, property and litigation – and there is some room for gaining experience in other areas of work. We have a full education programme running parallel with the practical training. There is a comprehensive range of departmental seminars and the firm has introduced a structured programme of skills training for assistants. These in-house courses all carry points towards complying with the Law Society's compulsory continuing education regulations and are managed by our Director of Education and Training.
For brochure and application form contact: Hugh Homan.

BERWIN LEIGHTON

Talented?

Responsive?

Articulate?

Inspired?

Natural?

Enterprising?

Enlightened?

Send for our brochure!

Contact: Hugh Homan
Staff Partner
Berwin Leighton
Solicitors
Adelaide House
London Bridge
London EC4R 9HA
Tel: 071-623 3144

S J Berwin & Co

Main office: 236 Gray's Inn Road, London WC1X 8HB. Tel: 071-278 0444; Fax: 071-833 2860; Telex: 8814928 WINLAW G.
Other offices: Brussels.
Senior Partner: C Haan.
Number of partners: 47
Number of staff: 345
Firm history: The firm was founded in 1982 by Stanley Berwin, a former senior director of N M Rothschild & Sons, and has expanded at a remarkable rate achieved by recruiting leading lawyers with a wide range of specialist disciplines. The firm's aim is to provide speedy and positive legal advice that is both commercial and practical, and regards a creative approach as essential.
Range of client services: The firm provides a full range of legal services to financial, industrial and commercial clients, both national and international, as well as advising private clients on trusts, tax planning and asset protection.

There are five main departments (corporate finance, commercial, litigation, property and tax) with expert teams working in particular areas. Although the firm is renowned for handling complex corporate transactions, it also specializes in EC and competition law, intellectual property, banking, securities law, commercial property, planning, media and entertainment law. Interdepartmental groups in the firm include insolvency, environmental and leisure.
Number of trainee solicitors required for 1994: 15 plus
Minimum academic requirements: Candidates must be of at least 2.1 ability but need not have read law.
Starting salary: £17,000 (September 1991).
Number of qualified solicitors required for 1992: In addition to trainee solicitors qualifying with the firm, qualified solicitor recruitment will be dictated by client demand.
Starting salary: £27,000 for newly qualified.
Annual leave entitlement: 20 days per annum.
Professional development policies and programmes: Education and training is led by our Director of Professional Development who, with the support of his team, brings together the expertise of partners, leading academics and other specialists to provide courses carefully integrated into the work of the practice and timed to coincide with the individual's career development.
Applications and brochure requests: Keith Wood (handwritten and CV).

Cameron Markby Hewitt

Main office: Sceptre Court, 40 Tower Hill, London EC3N 4BB. Tel: 071-702 2345; Fax: 071-702 2303.
Other offices: Bristol, Brussels, Lloyd's Building.
Senior Partner: Mr W T C Shelford.
Number of partners: 72
Number of staff: 550
Firm history: The firm results from the mergers of Cameron Markby, Hewitt Woollacott & Chown and Brafman Morris in May 1989 and is committed to continued growth. Major investment has been made in premises at Sceptre Court, providing an attractive environment including a new suite of training rooms and offering the latest generation information systems.
Range of client services: The firm acts for a wide range of national and multinational clients including banks, financial institutions, insurance brokers, trading corporations, media companies and professionals. We have a particular reputation in banking, insolvency, venture and development capital, entertainment, insurance litigation and commercial property work, and are recognized for our creative problem solving.
Number of trainee solicitors required for 1994: 35
Minimum academic requirements: A good honours degree, preferably 2.1 (law or non-law).
Starting salary: £17,000 (at September 1991) with reviews in March and September.
Number of qualified solicitors required for 1992: Although we retain over eighty per cent of our trainees on qualification we welcome applications from qualified solicitors.
Starting salary: £26,000 (at September 1991).
Annual leave entitlement: 20 working days, increasing with length of service.
Professional development policies and programmes: After an introductory training programme, our trainee solicitors spend up to six months in our five departments gaining comprehensive experience through working closely with their allocated partners and teams. Our overall aim is to provide a supportive but challenging environment, encouraging trainees to take on early responsibility. This is achieved through the provision of high quality work, regular reviews of trainees' performance, and their participation in legal and business seminars from the in-house training programme. Most trainee solicitors stay with the firm after qualification in the department of their choice. Once qualified, solicitors attend our professional development programme. The firm has recently won a National Training Award.
For brochure and application form contact: Christian Graham (qualified solicitors) or Helen Sheppard (trainee solicitors and vacation work).

Eversheds

Eversheds' national law practice has offices in thirteen commercial centres across England and Wales. The practice has a total complement of 1,700 people, including two hundred partners and offers the breadth and depth of legal advice normally only associated with a major London firm.

Eversheds was created in 1988, when six leading regional firms combined their resources to develop a national network of services and a jointly managed London practice.

With the ability to provide a wide range of specialist services through their regional offices, Eversheds' member firms are well placed to meet the increasingly diverse legal requirements of corporate clients. In future, this all-round capability will assume even greater importance as more and more nationally based organizations move their headquarters out of London.

Eversheds' working environment offers important benefits to young solicitors. Trainees can expect a variety and quality of work similar to that encountered in a big London firm, but with a level of individual attention that makes working in a regional firm so attractive. Through the resources of the national practice, also, they benefit from comprehensive training programmes, matched to their personal ambitions.

Offices, numbers of partners and staff:

Member	Locations	Partners	Total Staff
Alexander Tatham	Manchester Warrington	21	109
Daynes Hill & Perks	Norwich Great Yarmouth Ipswich	52	244
Evershed Wells & Hind	Birmingham Derby, Nottingham	55	469
Eversheds	London	9*	38
Hepworth & Chadwick	Leeds	27	280
Ingledew Botterell	Middlesbrough Newcastle	23	161
Phillips & Buck	Cardiff	22	200

*London partners are also partners of regional firms

Range of client services: Eversheds' member firms offer a complete range of services in five principal areas: corporate, commercial, litigation, property and private client work. In addition, by pooling expertise and resources, over thirty national specialist groups have been established to provide specialist legal advice on areas ranging from environmental law to fraud protection.

Number of trainee solicitors required for 1994: Approximately 76.

Minimum academic requirements: A good second class honours degree, although it need not be in law.

Trainee solicitors: Trainee solicitors can work in the office of their choice, and with Eversheds get the best of both worlds. The increased range of specialist advice that the clients demand, means that trainees get the quantity and quality of training needed to provide this. But they also get the individual attention from being in a smaller sized regional firm.

Professional development policies and programmes: The establishment of a comprehensive, unified training programme throughout Eversheds has been one of the practice's top priorities, and the Director of Training is responsible for devising training courses for all trainee solicitors, assistant solicitors and partners. Training also takes place through the national specialist groups at regular national conferences. The conference topics cover all the key areas of legal practice.

Eversheds' trainee solicitors gain experience in at least four different departments, under the direct supervision of a partner, and are trained in procedures for both disputed and undisputed cases.

For brochure and application form please write to the location of your choice:

Birmingham: Philip Williams, Evershed Wells & Hind, 10 Newhall Street, Birmingham B3 3LX. Tel: 021-233 2001.

Cardiff: Louise Huzzey, Phillips & Buck, Fitzalan House, Fitzalan Road, Cardiff CF2 1XZ. Tel: 0222-471147.

Leeds: Robert Chapman, Hepworth & Chadwick, Cloth Hall Court, Infirmary Street, Leeds LS1 2JB. Tel: 0532-430391.

London: Lou Putley, 1 Gunpowder Square, Printer Street, London EC4A 3DE. Tel: 071-936 2553.

Manchester: Janet Knowles, Alexander Tatham, 30 St Ann Street, Manchester M2 3DB. Tel: 061-236 4444.

Newcastle: Stephen Mills, Ingledew Botterell, Milburn House, Dean Street, Newcastle upon Tyne NE1 1NP. Tel: 091-261 1661.

Norwich: Chris Gilham, Daynes Hill & Perks, Holland Court, The Close, Norwich NR1 4DX. Tel: 0603-611212.

Nottingham: Carole Wigley, Evershed Wells & Hind, 14 Fletcher Gate, Nottingham NG1 2FX. Tel: 0602-506201.

THE IVANHOE GUIDE
ORDER FORM

Please supply the following Ivanhoe Guides:

☐	The Ivanhoe Guide to Chartered Accountants 1992	£7.95
☐	The Ivanhoe Guide to Pensions Management 1992	£7.95
☐	The Ivanhoe Guide to the Banking and Securities Industry 1992	£7.95
☐	The Ivanhoe Guide to Management Consultants 1992	£7.95
☐	The Ivanhoe Guide to Insurance 1992	£7.95
☐	The Ivanhoe Guide to Actuaries 1992	£9.95
☐	The Ivanhoe Guide to Chartered Patent Agents 1992	£7.95
☐	The Ivanhoe/Blackstone Guide to the Legal Profession 1992	£9.95
☐	The Ivanhoe Guide to Chartered Surveyors 1992	£7.95
☐	The Ivanhoe Guide to the Engineering Profession 1992	£9.95

Name:..

Address:..

....

.... Postcode:........................

....

Please enclose cheque with order, including postage and packing as follows: 1 copy £1.50; 2 to 5 copies £3 – or take to your local bookshop.

Charles Letts & Co Ltd, Letts of London House, Parkgate Road, London SW11 4NQ. Tel: 071-407 8891.

Frere Cholmeley

Main office: 28 Lincoln's Inn Fields, London WC2A 3HH. Tel: 071-405 7878; Fax: 071-405 9056.
Other offices: Paris, Rome, Milan, Barcelona, Brussels, Monte Carlo, Berlin.
Chairman: Bruce Brodie.
Chief Executive: Tim Razzall.
Number of partners: 50 (151 qualified lawyers including partners).
Number of staff: 401
Firm history: Founded in 1750. Since the 1950s Frere Cholmeley has developed its comprehensive corporate and commercial practice both in the UK and overseas and it is now one of the leading European law firms. The Paris office was opened in 1968, Monte Carlo in 1979, Milan in 1988, Brussels and Berlin in 1990, and Rome and Barcelona in 1991.
Range of client services: The *company and commercial department* advises on all aspects of corporate finance and banking, undertaking major transactional work for listed and non-listed clients. The *litigation department* has experience in all areas of commercial litigation and a high proportion of its work has an international element; the Anglo-German group strengthens the international team. Other cross-department groups include aviation, environmental, employment, entertainment and tax. The *property department* has a broad practice in commercial development and planning work, working with major international property organizations. The *private client department* offers an extensive range of services to individual clients.
Number of trainee solicitors required for 1994: 25
Minimum academic requirements: Law and non-law graduates with 2.1 ability.
Starting salary: £17,000
Number of qualified solicitors required for 1992: 20-25
Starting salary: £26,000 (1991 qualifiers).
Annual leave entitlement: 20 working days plus additional leave at Christmas. Increases with time at firm.
Professional development policies and programmes: The firm has a training officer who is responsible for the continuing education programme. This includes departmental seminars and lectures given by internal and external speakers on a wide range of legal topics. In addition, there are lectures on non-legal topics related to the City and other business subjects. Trainee solicitors also receive practical and communication skills training.
For brochure contact: Paul Roberts. A brochure is available to inform applicants about articles at Frere Cholmeley. Application by letter and full CV.

Herbert Smith

Main office: Exchange House, Primrose Street, London EC2A 2HS. Tel: 071-374 8000; Fax: 071-496 0043.
Overseas offices: Brussels, Hong Kong, New York and Paris.
Overseas links: Links with lawyers throughout the world.
Senior Partner: John Rowson.
Number of partners: 94
Number of staff: 965
Firm history: Herbert Smith was founded in 1882 by Norman Herbert Smith. It has grown particularly rapidly in recent years and we moved to new offices in London in 1990. Our growth is the result of the effort of all those working at Herbert Smith and not the result of a merger with another firm.
Firm structure: Herbert Smith is organized into groups of partners and qualified lawyers together with trainees in order to give a top level of service to clients in all aspects of commercial work, much of it international. The work often involves close coordination between experts in different fields, with significant involvement of overseas clients and lawyers.

An example of our commitment to the future is the development of our own information data base to which each fee earner (including each trainee solicitor) has access from the computer terminal and screen on his or her desk.

Trainee solicitors are given experience in a wide range of the firm's work.
Range of client services: Herbert Smith provides a full range of services to cover all aspects of UK and international commercial work.
Number of trainee solicitors required for 1994: Approximately 60.
Minimum academic requirements: Herbert Smith welcomes applications from those with non-law degrees as well as those who are studying law. Candidates will need to be bright and able to use their own initiative. They will also be people who will be able to understand and deal with clients and be able to take significant responsibility.
Starting salary: Herbert Smith provides an excellent remuneration package (including bursaries during years spent studying for the Law Society exams).
Opportunities for qualified solicitors: We are always looking for bright people who are anxious to be involved in top quality work.
Annual leave entitlement: 22 days per year.
Training: Training and information are vital at all stages of a legal career. In addition to the practical experience of working on top quality matters, Herbert Smith provides a full range of in-house training programmes for both trainee solicitors and all its qualified lawyers.
For brochure and application form contact: Patrick Robinson.

Map Your Future

Training with Herbert Smith opens up all sorts of opportunities in the law. The range of our practice means that our trainee solicitors have broad experience and, on qualifying, have a wide variety of long term career paths open to them.

The work of a City lawyer involves judgment as well as legal ability. For example in the balancing of conflicting interests, whether concerning an international corporate rescue or a family company dispute.

We are looking for bright people and it does not matter whether or not you are working for a law degree.

In a time of unprecedented change for the legal profession, both in the UK and in Europe, there will be excellent opportunities for bright lawyers with leading law firms.

HERBERT SMITH

Patrick Robinson, Recruitment Partner, Exchange House, Primrose Street, London EC2A 2HS. Tel: 071 374 8000

LONDON • BRUSSELS • HONG KONG • NEW YORK • PARIS

Lovell White Durrant

Main office: 65 Holborn Viaduct, London EC1A 2DY. Tel: 071-236 0066; Fax: 071-248 4212/071-236 0084.
Other offices and links: New York, Paris, Brussels, Prague, Hong Kong, Beijing, Tokyo.
Senior Partner: Cavan Taylor.
Number of partners: 124
Number of staff: 1,300
Range of client services: The firm provides a full range of services to the business client. The principal areas of advice are: banking; commercial and private company; computers and telecommunications; construction and engineering; corporate finance; corporate tax, EC and competition law; employment, industrial relations and pensions; energy; environmental law; financial services; insolvency; insurance and reinsurance; intellectual property; international trade; investigations and inquiries; investment funds; litigation and arbitration; media law; planning and rating; private client and tax planning; product liability; property; shipping; venture capital and management buy-outs.
Number of trainee solicitors required for 1994: 80
Minimum academic requirements: Law and non-law graduates (particularly scientists, engineers and linguists). Candidates must be of 2.1 calibre.
Starting salary: £17,000 per annum (reviewed 1st March 1992). Financial assistance provided for both CPE and Law Finals courses.
Annual leave entitlement: 22 days per year.
Training: In addition to practical training provided by day-to-day working with partners and senior solicitors, a full in-house training programme is provided for all trainee solicitors and qualified staff.
For brochure and application form contact: Mrs Lynda Neal, Lovell White Durrant, 65 Holborn Viaduct, London EC1A 2DY. Tel: 071-236 0066.

International Practice at large

From one of the very largest City firms, our clients expect strength in depth. And rightly. The capacity to respond at once; to field the right team in the numbers they need.

We think that strength in breadth is an asset too. Not just for our clients but for all of us - especially our trainees.

Ours is a practice with many diverse specialities and a range of expertise across the board. From EEC law to asset recovery. From corporate finance to intellectual property.

If you would like to know more about our work and training with us, apply to:

Lynda Neal,
Lovell White Durrant,
65 Holborn Viaduct,
London EC1A 2DY

BANKING
COMMERCIAL & PRIVATE COMPANY
COMPUTERS & TELECOMMUNICATIONS
CONSTRUCTION & ENGINEERING
CORPORATE FINANCE
CORPORATE TAX
EEC & COMPETITION LAW
EMPLOYMENT & INDUSTRIAL RELATIONS
ENERGY
ENVIRONMENTAL LAW
FINANCIAL SERVICES
INSOLVENCY
INSURANCE & REINSURANCE
INTELLECTUAL PROPERTY
INTERNATIONAL TRADE
INVESTIGATIONS & INQUIRIES
INVESTMENT FUNDS
LITIGATION & ARBITRATION
MEDIA LAW
PENSIONS
PLANNING & RATING
PRIVATE CLIENT & TAX PLANNING
PRODUCT LIABILITY
PROPERTY
SHIPPING
VENTURE CAPITAL & MANAGEMENT BUY-OUTS

LONDON   NEW YORK   PARIS   BRUSSELS   PRAGUE   HONG KONG   BEIJING   TOKYO

Nabarro Nathanson

Main office: 50 Stratton Street, London W1X 5FL. Tel: 071-493 9933; Fax: 071-629 7900 DX No: 77.
Regional offices: Doncaster and Hull.
Senior Partner: Jeffrey Greenwood.
Number of partners: 105
Number of staff: 800
Firm history: Nabarro Nathanson was formed in 1958 from the merger of two older established Piccadilly firms, whose origins date back to the beginning of this century. Our present offices in Stratton Street, near St James, are conveniently located for clients in the City and Central London, and for the convenience of our clients in the North of England we have regional offices in Doncaster and Hull. We have grown dramatically over the years in order to meet the continuing growth in demand of our services. Our international network of associations has expanded and we have now established branch offices in Hungary, Poland and Dubai.
Range of client services: The majority of our work is in the commercial field; our clients range from one-man companies to multinationals and governments. We have specialist departments handling a wide range of commercial work: corporate, property, litigation, tax and trusts, pensions, construction, public sector and planning. We also have teams working in banking and finance, EC and environmental, share incentives, insolvency and intellectual property. International work is undertaken by the majority of these departments.
Number of trainee solicitors required for 1994: 30 in London, 6 in Northern offices.
Minimum academic requirements: Applicants must be of 2.1 ability, not necessarily with a degree in law.
Starting salary: London: £17,000 (May 1991) rising in stages to £19,750 in the last six months of articles; Northern offices: £12,750 (September 1991) rising in stages to £15,250 in the last six months of articles. These figures are reviewed every six months to maintain competitiveness.
Annual leave entitlement: 20 working days plus extra as service lengthens.
Professional development policies and programmes: Our trainee solicitors are involved in a comprehensive training programme organized by the Director of Legal Education. We have made legal, business and personal skills a major priority and are well-known for our coherent and integrated training strategy which is complemented by our dedicated training centre. There are opportunities to work overseas for qualified lawyers, and we have an active programme to develop associations worldwide.
For trainee solicitors' brochure and application form contact: Ms Pat Haynes, Director of Personnel.

A PARTICULAR KIND OF TRAINEE SOLICITOR

 The type of law firm you choose depends on the type of person you are.

You are intelligent and have a lively inquiring mind. You sense that you would give your best in a professional but informal and relaxed atmosphere. You are considering law as a career but feel your outgoing personality may not be compatible with what you perceive law firms to be.

If we have described you here, we have also described a Nabarro Nathanson person.

We are one of the UK's leading law practices with offices in London, Doncaster, and Hull, and our range of specialist departments offers scope for variety in articles and a challenging career.

Our refreshing approach demands the highest professional standards and the pursuit of excellence. Individual efforts are recognised and well-rewarded and we encourage our trainees to take on as much responsibility as their talents and experience will allow.

If you like what you have read so far, come along and see for yourself how different we are.

We offer top salaries and are interested in high calibre graduates (not necessarily with a degree in law).

Telephone or write to: Pat Haynes, Director of Personnel.

NABARRO NATHANSON
50 Stratton Street, London W1X 5FL
Telephone: 071-493 9933

A Particular Kind of Law Firm

REGULATED IN THE CONDUCT OF INVESTMENT BUSINESS BY THE LAW SOCIETY

Slaughter and May

Main office: 35 Basinghall Street, London EC2V 5DB. Tel: 071-600 1200; Fax: 071-726 0038/071-600 0289; Telex: 883486/888926.
Other offices: London, Paris, Brussels, Frankfurt, Hong Kong, Tokyo, New York.
Senior Partner: G B Inglis.
Number of partners: 97 worldwide.
Number of staff: 1,250 worldwide.
Firm history: The firm celebrated its centenary in 1989; its founders William Slaughter and William May quickly established a thriving practice in the City, the demand for their services resulting from the combination of excellence in legal technique and practical common sense. That tradition has been followed ever since, both in the UK and overseas, new demands being met by new skills and services. The international work has been a feature from the start.
Range of client services: The great majority of work is in the commercial field; our clients range from one-man companies to multinationals and governments. We meet all their needs in commercial law except admiralty. Complementing the firm's main activities in the corporate and financial field are the vital specialist departments including litigation/arbitration, property, tax, pensions/employment, EC/competition, financial services and intellectual property. We can put a team together on any transaction because of this breadth of expertise (and our services are available throughout the world).
Number of trainee solicitors required for 1994: 75 (approximately).
Minimum academic requirements: Candidates must be of 2.1 ability but do not need to have read law.
Starting salary: £17,250 (May 1991) rising in stages to £20,700 in the last six months of articles. On qualifying, £27,000.
Annual leave entitlement: 22 working days.
Professional development policies and programmes: It is the firm's policy to meet all challenges and changes through forward planning, good training (carried out principally by our own professional training staff) and new specialist skills where necessary. We aim to maintain an outstanding team of people who enjoy working together. Even though we are one of the largest firms, quality is more important than quantity; size alone is not enough.
Applications and enquiries should be made in writing to: Neil Morgan, Head of Personnel.

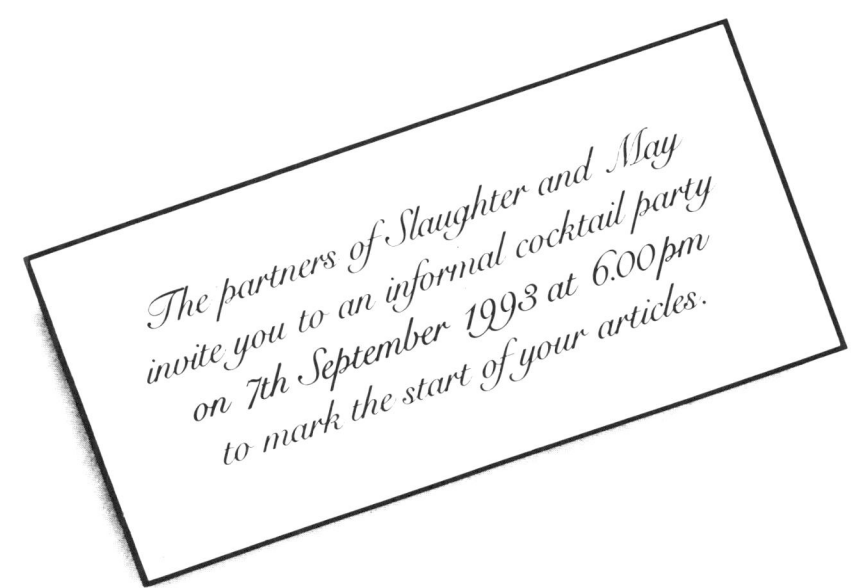

Even on your first day you will be staying late.

After signing your Articles with Slaughter and May you will need to work hard to succeed.

However, you will find we work just as hard at ensuring your efforts are rewarded.

Our success has been based on giving individuals an environment which allows their different talents to develop and also recognises their achievements.

That way we know they will give their best. It is also the way we have come to advise some of the world's biggest companies.

Our selection process is individual in its approach.

We welcome graduates of at least 2.1 standard from any discipline, not just Law. If you have the personality, intellect and common sense to be 'part of the team', then you are probably right for Slaughter and May.

For more details on how to apply for articles, please write to Neil Morgan, Head of Personnel, Slaughter and May, 35 Basinghall Street, London EC2V 5DB.

SLAUGHTER AND MAY

LONDON · PARIS · HONG KONG · NEW YORK · TOKYO · BRUSSELS

AN INTERNATIONAL FIRM WITH AN INDIVIDUAL APPROACH.

Taylor Willcocks

Main office: 23 London Road, Croydon CR9 2RE. Tel: 081-681 5544; Fax: 081-681 2745.
Other offices: Wallington, Cheam and Streatham.
Senior Partner: Colin Stone.
Number of partners: 5
Number of staff: 30
History: Taylor Willcocks opened its first office in the Strand in London in 1901, the Cheam office was opened in the 1930s and Wallington during the 1950s. More recently the firm has acquired offices in Streatham and in Croydon.
Range of client services: Taylor Willcocks conducts an extensive general practice across North Surrey and South London including a wide range of private client and commercial work, property, litigation, tax and trusts and financial services.
Number of trainee solicitors required for 1994: 3
Minimum academic requirements: 2.2 degree but this need not necessarily be in law, and the firm considers personal qualities to be equally as important as academic achievement.
Starting salary: Negotiable.
Annual leave entitlement: 20 days plus Bank Holidays.
For brochure and application form contact: Paul Trim – Tel: 081-647 8133.

Titmuss Sainer & Webb

Main office: 2 Serjeants' Inn, London EC4Y 1LT. Tel: 071-583 5353; Fax: 071-353 3683/2830 DX 30 London; Telex: 23823 ADVICE G.
Senior Partner: Michael Smith.
Chief Executive: Michael Reid.
Number of partners: 45
Number of staff: 300
Firm history, range of client services: Titmuss Sainer & Webb is one of the City's leading medium sized commercial firms, highly regarded for the quality of its work, innovative training and friendly working environment. The firm is organized into corporate, property and litigation departments and specialist multidisciplinary teams handling commercial, banking, insolvency, employment, taxation, construction and planning and rating law. Our clients include UK and overseas-based listed and private companies from a wide cross section of industry and commerce. We are committed to further well-planned growth and to the constant development of our resources, skills and training initiatives to build upon our very favourable position in the market for legal services.
Number of trainee solicitors required for 1994: 15–20
Minimum academic requirements: Second-class degree.
Starting salary: £16,500 (September 1991).
Professional development policies and programmes: Trainee solicitors are given every opportunity to gain a broad knowledge of commercial law. Recruitment is limited in order to give the fullest attention to training and career development and allow direct client contact and responsibility at an early stage. Articles are divided into six four-monthly periods; eight months in a department is often split into four months' general work followed by four months' specialization in a unit of the trainee's choice. Training is essentially practical but seminars and courses, including instruction in management matters, are organized and coordinated throughout articles by our full-time Director of Training, Judith Mayhew.

Titmuss Sainer & Webb is at a particularly exciting stage in its development. It is large enough to offer full team support and sophisticated back up and administration – small enough to allow trainee solicitors to make their mark and play a significant role in its future: a firm which we hope they, like the majority of our past trainees, will enjoy remaining with after qualification. The firm also offers a limited number of final-year students an opportunity to join the summer vacation visit scheme.
For brochure and application form contact: Judith Mayhew.

Turner Kenneth Brown

Main office: 100 Fetter Lane, London EC4A 1DD. Tel: 071-242 6006; Fax: 071-242 3003.
Other UK offices: Abbot's House, Abbey Street, Reading RG1 3BD. Tel: 0734-504700; Fax: 0734-505640.
Overseas offices and links: Brussels, Dubai (associate), Hong Kong, Prague.
Senior Partner: David R Wightman.
Number of partners: 63
Number of other staff: 364
Firm history: Although it can trace its history back over 200 years, the firm is very forward looking. In 1983, the twenty-nine partners in the law firms of Kenneth Brown Baker Baker and Turner Peacock merged to form Turner Kenneth Brown. The further merger in 1989 with the long established City firm of Lawrance Messer & Co, heralded another stage in its development as a major City firm. Since then, the firm has opened offices in Hong Kong, Brussels, Prague and the M4 corridor at Reading.

In 1990, the firm announced a formal alliance with Thelan, Marrin, Johnson & Bridges of the United States. The alliance combines the capabilities of TKB's 213 lawyers with Thelen's 350 lawyers and is the latest step towards its goal of becoming a truly multinational firm.

Firm structure: The firm has the following main departments: company/commercial, property, litigation, private client, taxation, and intellectual property/information technology. In addition there are a number of less formal groups dealing either with specific areas of law (eg employment and immigration) or with particular types of industry/market sector (eg construction/engineering, charities, the health sector, computers and communications, and financial institutions).
Number of trainee solicitors required for 1994: Approximately 30.
Minimum academic requirements: 2.2 degree (not necessarily in law).
Starting salary: £17,000 (October 1991).
Number of qualified solicitors required for 1992: No upper or lower limit but probably around 30 (including qualifying trainee solicitors).
Starting salary: Negotiable.
Annual leave: Four weeks (plus extra day at Christmas and Easter).
Professional development policies and programmes: TKB has established an extensive training and development programme for trainee solicitors, assistant solicitors and partners using a combination of in-house training, Law Society and other external training courses.
For brochure and application form contact: Personnel Manager, Turner Kenneth Brown, Fetter Lane, London EC4A 1DD.

Watson, Farley & Williams

Main office: 15 Appold Street, London EC2A 2HB. Tel: 071-814 8000; Fax: 071-814 8141; Telex: 8955707.
Overseas offices: France – Paris; Norway – Oslo; and (through an international partnership) USA – New York; Greece – Athens.
Senior Partner: Alastair Farley.
Number of partners: 32
Number of staff: 258
Firm history and structure: The firm was established in the City of London in 1982 and has expanded rapidly into an international commercial law practice. Its expertise in a number of specialist areas enables it to compete successfully with the largest City firms for high quality work. Lawyers are encouraged to work across traditional departmental boundaries and the firm places an emphasis on training its solicitors to become good all-round commercial lawyers before they specialize in any particular area.
Recent major events: In October 1991, the London office moved to new premises near Broadgate.
Range of client services: The principal areas of practice of the firm are: shipping and ship finance including oil and gas work, banking, asset finance and insolvency work, aviation and aircraft finance, corporate and commercial including corporate finance, intellectual property and employment, litigation, taxation, EC and competition and commercial property.
Number of trainee solicitors required for 1994: 12
Minimum academic requirements: Second class honours degree, not necessarily in law.
Starting salary: £17,250 (September 1991).
Number of qualified solicitors required for 1992: The practice continues to grow and applications are welcomed from good quality candidates in all the firm's practice areas.
Starting salary: Negotiable.
Annual leave entitlement: 20 days.
Professional development policies and programmes: New trainees are introduced to the firm with an induction course covering legal topics and practical instruction. The firm has a full continuing education programme, run in conjunction with academics from leading universities, for all trainees and qualified solicitors. Trainees spend time in at least four areas of the firm's practice, becoming involved in transactions at an early stage, and many trainees are able to spend some time in one of the overseas offices.
For brochure and application form contact: William Bale, Partnership Secretary.

Wilde Sapte

Main office: Queensbridge House, 60 Upper Thames Street, London EC4V 3BD. Tel: 071-236 3050; Fax: 071-236 9624; Telex: 887793 WILDES G.
Other offices and links: The firm has full service offices in New York and Brussels and extensive links with other law firms throughout the world.
Senior Partner: Charles Leeming.
Managing Partner: Philip Brown.
Number of partners: 55
Number of staff: 470 (of which 120 are assistant solicitors and 60 are trainee solicitors).
Firm history: Founded in 1785, Wilde Sapte is a leading City commercial practice, representing both UK and overseas clients on a worldwide basis. The firm has expanded rapidly in recent years, doubling in size since 1983. We have developed close working relationships with other international law firms and professions in every major financial centre throughout the world in order to meet clients' needs wherever they arise. In addition, Wilde Sapte has extensive professional contacts in the Middle and Far East. We offer exchange schemes with leading firms in Europe and Japan, and secondments with the European Commission.
Firm structure: The firm comprises six departments – banking and finance, company and commercial, litigation, property, corporate tax, and institutional services. The largest departments are further subdivided into specialist groups, dealing with specific areas of commercial work. In addition, we have Spanish and Japanese speaking units within the firm to serve the particular needs of clients from, or with interests in, those countries. We believe this structure helps us to serve our clients' needs in the most efficient and reliable manner. However, we remain flexible and often assemble hand picked teams for particular tasks, drawing on the firm's resources as a whole.
Major events in the past year: Wilde Sapte has undergone rapid development recently and is committed to growth to enable it to take advantage of the opportunities offered by 1992 and developments within the profession. The firm has continued to strengthen its intellectual property, construction, tax and corporate finance departments. In addition, the firm's outside profile has been significantly raised through its programme of seminars giving major briefings on important areas of business.
Range of client services: The *banking and finance department* offers general banking and financial documentation services, including consumer credit, capital markets, corporate reconstructions, aviation and shipping finance, project finance, and trade finance.

The *company and commercial department* offers a full range of services to UK and international public and private companies and to their financial advisers,

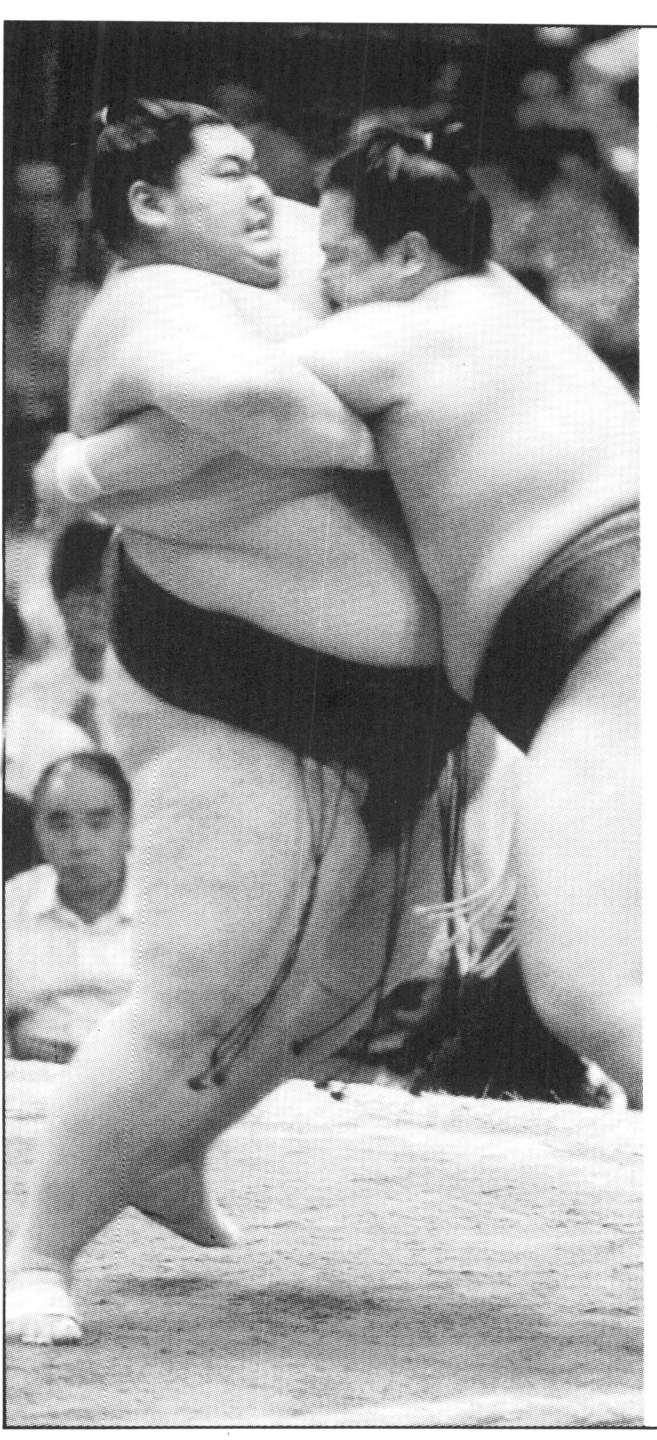

We won't take your training lightly

WILDE SAPTE
—

*If you would like
to find out more about us,
pick up our recruitment brochure from your
careers service, or contact our Personnel Director
David Fowler at the address below:*

Queensbridge House
60 Upper Thames Street
London EC4V 3BD
Telephone 071 236 3050

including the formation of companies, joint ventures, flotations and mergers and acquisitions.

The *litigation department* consists of over eighty solicitors and other professional staff who handle all aspects of commercial litigation, often international in scope. The department deals with disputes in a number of specialist areas such as construction, banking and finance, insolvency, shipping, aviation, trade, employment and insurance.

The *commercial property department* handles a broad range of work for major companies and institutional clients including the acquisition and disposal of properties, secured lending, planning, institutional investment and joint ventures. The transactions often have significant tax or accounting implications.

Our *corporate tax department*, one of the fastest growing in the firm, works closely with clients' internal tax departments and provides an integrated support service to our other departments.

Finally, the *institutional services department* deals with pension schemes and advice, charities, UK and international trusts, and immigration law.

Number of trainee solicitors required for 1994: Approximately 36.
Minimum academic requirements: A good degree, although not necessarily in law.
Starting salary: £17,000 (September 1991).
Number of qualified solicitors required for 1992: We are always interested in applications from well-qualified solicitors.
Starting salary: £26,000 – newly qualified solicitors (September 1991).
Annual leave entitlement: 20 working days plus extra as service lengthens.
Professional development policies and programmes: It is our policy to invest in broad and well-structured training for all new recruits at whatever level in order to guarantee the firm's future success. Our director of education oversees this. Trainees receive a full induction course including documents and skills training, and 'The City' course which shows how the major institutions work and explains the terminology. There is also a programme of continuing education for everyone through regular seminars and lectures.
For brochure and application form contact: David Fowler, Director of Personnel. Tel: 071-236 3050.